Graceful Beginnings Series

for New-to-the-Bible Christians

Grace Overflowing

The Joy of Christ in Your Life
(A Study of Paul's Letters)

MELANIE NEWTON

JOYFUL
WALK
BIBLE
STUDIES

For questions about the use of this study guide, please visit www.melanienewton.com to contact us.

ISBN: 978-0-9978703-3-6

Cover design and study layout by Melanie Newton. Cover photo by John Newton. The map graphic used in each lesson is from www.thebiblejourney.org. The "Grace Overflowing" image is a freely accessible online image.

Melanie Newton specializes in Lifestyle Disciplemaking training to equip women to share their faith through casual conversation and disciple new believers. She also offers *Joyful Walk Bible Studies* for women at www.melanienewton.com.

We pray that you will find the *Graceful Beginnings Series* books to be a resource that God will use to strengthen you in your faith walk with Him.

JOYFUL WALK PRESS
Flower Mound, TX

MELANIE NEWTON

Melanie Newton is a Louisiana girl who made the choice to follow Jesus while attending LSU. She and her husband Ron married and moved to Texas for him to attend Dallas Theological Seminary. They stayed in Texas where Ron led a wilderness camping ministry for troubled youth for many years. He now helps corporations with their challenging employees. Melanie jumped into raising three Texas-born children and serving in ministry to women at her church.

Through the years, the Lord has given her opportunity to do Bible teaching and to write grace-based Bible studies for women that are now available from her website (melanienewton.com) and on Bible.org.

Melanie is currently a disciplemaking trainer—equipping and encouraging Christian women everywhere to pursue a lifestyle of disciplemaking. Her heart's desire is to encourage you to have a joyful relationship with Jesus Christ so you are willing to share that experience with others around you.

"Jesus took hold of me in 1972, and I've been on this great adventure ever since. My life is a gift of God, full of blessings in the midst of difficult challenges. The more I've learned and experienced God's absolutely amazing grace, the more I've discovered my faith walk to be a joyful one. I'm still seeking that joyful walk every day..."

Melanie

OTHER BIBLE STUDIES BY MELANIE NEWTON

Graceful Beginnings Series books for new-to-the-Bible Christians:

A Fresh Start

Painting the Portrait of Jesus

The God You Can Know

Grace Overflowing

Joyful Walk Bible Studies for growing Christians:

Graceful Living: The Essentials of Living a Grace-Based Christian Life

7 Cs of a Firm Foundation: A Study Based on Genesis 1-11

Everyday Women, Ever Faithful God: Old Testament Women

Profiles of Perseverance: Old Testament Men

Live Out His Love: New Testament Women

Radical Acts: Adventure with the Spirit from the Book of Acts

Knowing Jesus, Knowing Joy: A Study of Philippians

Healthy Living: A Study of Colossians

Adorn Yourself with Godliness: A Study of 1 Timothy and Titus

Perspective: A Study of 1 and 2 Thessalonians

To Be Found Faithful: A Study of 2 Timothy

Find these and more resources for your spiritual growth at melanienewton.com.

Contents

Introduction 1

Paul and His Letters.................................... 9

The Letter to the Romans 21

The First Corinthians Letter 29

The Second Corinthians Letter................ 37

The Letter to the Galatians..................... 47

The Letter to the Ephesians 57

The Letter to the Philippians................... 67

The Letter to the Colossians.................... 75

The First and Second Letters to the Thessalonians 83

The First Letter to Timothy..................... 93

The Second Letter to Timothy 103

The Letter to Titus................................ 113

The Letter to Philemon......................... 121

A Quick Look at Paul's Letters............... 129

GRACE
OVERFLOWING   Introduction

"The grace of our Lord was poured out on me abundantly, along with the faith and love that are in Christ Jesus." (1 Timothy 1:14)

GRACEFUL BEGINNINGS

The *Graceful Beginnings Series* of Bible studies are specifically designed for the new-to-the-Bible Christian—whether you are a new Christian or you just feel insecure about understanding the Bible. The lessons are basic, introducing you as an inexperienced Christian to your God and His way of approaching life in simple terms that can be easily understood.

Just as a newborn baby needs to know the love and trustworthiness of her parents, the new Christian needs to know and experience the love and trustworthiness of her God. *A Fresh Start* is the first book in the series, laying a good foundation of truth for you to grasp and apply to your life. The other books in the series can be done in any order.

SOME BIBLE BASICS

Throughout these lessons, you will use a Bible to answer questions as you discover treasure about your life with Christ. The Bible is one book containing a collection of 66 books combined together for our benefit. It is divided into two main parts: the Old Testament and the New Testament.

The Old Testament tells the story of the beginning of the world and God's promises to mankind given through the nation of Israel. It tells how the people of Israel obeyed and disobeyed God over many, many years. All the stories and messages in the Old Testament lead up to Jesus Christ's coming to the earth.

The New Testament tells the story of Jesus Christ, the early Christians, and God's promises to all those who believe in Jesus. You can think of the Old Testament as "before Christ" and the New Testament as "after Christ."

Each book of the Bible is divided into chapters and verses within those chapters to make it easier to study. Bible references include the book name, chapter number and verse number(s). For example, Ephesians 2:8 refers to the New Testament book of Ephesians, the 2nd chapter, and verse 8 within that 2nd chapter. Printed Bibles have a "Table of Contents" in the front to help you locate books by page number. Bible apps also have a contents list by book and chapter.

The Bible verses highlighted at the beginning of each lesson in this study are from the New International Version® (NIV®) unless otherwise indicated. You can use any version of the Bible to answer the questions, but using a more easy-to-read translation (NIRV, NLT, NET, ESV) will help you gain confidence in understanding what you are reading. You can find all these translations in the "YouVersion App" or on www.biblegateway.com.

This study capitalizes certain pronouns referring to God, Jesus and the Holy Spirit—He, Him, His, Himself—just to make the reading of the study information less confusing. Some Bible translations likewise capitalize those pronouns referring to God; others do not. It is simply a matter of preference, not a requirement.

A map is included in each lesson so you can follow Paul's journeys, see where he was when he wrote each letter, and see where the receiving church or individual was located.

GRACE OVERFLOWING

The *Grace Overflowing* lessons will give you an overview of the thirteen letters of Paul found in the New Testament. Paul was a very well-educated and devout Jew and the author of more of the New Testament than anyone else. Jesus chose him to be an apostle to non-Jews everywhere, to teach the message of God's grace to them. And, Paul understood God's grace overflowing to his life so well because he desperately needed it.

In the first letter he wrote to his close friend Timothy, Paul describes how he had experienced God's grace overflowing to his life.

> *I thank Christ Jesus our Lord, who has given me strength, that he considered me trustworthy, appointing me to his service. Even though I was once a blasphemer and a persecutor and a violent man, I was shown mercy because I acted in ignorance*

and unbelief. **The grace of our Lord was poured out on me abundantly**, *along with the faith and love that are in Christ Jesus. Here is a trustworthy saying that deserves full acceptance: Christ Jesus came into the world to save sinners— of whom I am the worst. But for that very reason I was shown mercy so that in me, the worst of sinners,* **Christ Jesus might display** *his immense patience as an example for those who would believe in him and receive eternal life. Now to the King eternal, immortal, invisible, the only God, be honor and glory forever and ever. Amen. (1 Timothy 1:12-17)*

The Apostle Paul exclaimed that God's grace is so abundant that it's like a vessel overflowing or a stream overflowing a waterfall into a pool below. It covers and fills whatever is around and beneath it. The Apostle Paul looked at his own history, which was filled with horrid behavior, filled with what many would consider unforgivable deeds. You may have thought of your own life in that way.

Yet, God's chose to extend His grace to Paul and show him mercy. Not just a little bit of grace. Abundant grace. Overflowing grace. Paul didn't deserve anything but punishment and shame. God's grace overcame that. **God's grace is His undeserved favor abundantly poured out on those who desperately need Him.** It is God giving favor to someone, not because they are good enough to deserve it but because His love chooses to do so. God chooses to have His grace overflowing to every believer from the moment of salvation. And, we continue to receive God's abundant grace throughout our lives on earth.

You received this grace overflowing to your life the moment you trusted in Jesus Christ. And, God's grace is overflowing to your life every day because you are in Christ.

Paul's life was changed from the inside out. He became a beacon of Christ's life shining through his own life. Christ displayed Himself through Paul's life because grace overflowed into his life. Paul understood God's grace so well because he desperately needed it for life.

The New Testament contains 13 of Paul's letters. Eight of these letters Paul wrote to churches that he had started or had strongly influenced. He wrote five letters specifically to individuals—pastors and church leaders. Through the *Grace Overflowing* lessons, you will become familiar with the people receiving each letter, the challenges they were facing (similar to our own), and the "grace-overflowing" solutions God gave to them (and to us) through Paul.

In his letters, Paul presents **Christ as everything we need for life**. Our God wants us to learn to live dependently on His Son as we live out our daily lives. Paul teaches us how to do this through his letters. These lessons do not cover each letter in detail, but you will learn a simple phrase describing how each letter presents Christ as the answer to specific needs we have and how He meets those needs in our lives as we trust in Him to do it.

Trust Him to meet your needs. His grace overflowing to your life.

LIVING DEPENDENTLY ON CHRIST

At the end of each lesson, we will include three things to help you make a fresh start in the right direction: "Bible verse to learn," "Response in prayer & praise," and "Getting to know Him more" readings.

1) Bible verse to learn

To renew your thinking and make part of your life as you journey on this adventure. Memorizing Bible verses is not just something "to do." You are planting God's words to you in your mind. The Bible calls it "renewing your mind" with truth about who God is and who you are.

If your Bible is a different translation from the one given in *Grace Overflowing,* feel free to memorize the verse from your Bible rather than what is given. The point is to begin a habit of memorizing Scripture. You will be surprised at how soon it just flows from your mind.

2) Response in prayer & praise

To help you begin regular conversation with your God who loves you dearly.

You will be encouraged to talk to God about anything and everything. Tell Him what you are thinking and feeling. He is someone you can trust.

You will be encouraged to praise God for who He is and what He does. Praise is appreciation of God and giving Him credit for who He is.

3) Getting to know Him more

Bible reading of selected portions of Paul's letters highlighting what it means to live as a Christian and experience God's grace overflowing to your life.

Spend a few minutes each day reading these wonderful letters and reflecting on how God's marvelous grace offers you a life of freedom and joy.

WHAT YOU WILL LEARN

The thirteen lessons in *Grace Overflowing* will cover these truths for you to know:

✓ ROMANS: Christ is our righteousness.

"This righteousness from God comes through faith in Jesus Christ to all who believe." Romans 3:22 (NIV)

✓ 1 CORINTHIANS: Christ is the wisdom of God.

"but to those whom God has called, both Jews and Greeks, Christ the power of God and the wisdom of God." (1 Corinthians 1:24 NIV)

✓ 2 CORINTHIANS: Christ is our comforter.

*"Praise be to the God and Father of our Lord Jesus Christ, the Father of compassion and the God of all **comfort**, who **comforts** us in all our troubles, so that we can **comfort** those in any trouble with the **comfort** we ourselves receive from God." (2 Corinthians 1:3-4 NIV)*

✓ GALATIANS: Christ is our freedom from the law.

"My brothers and sisters, you were chosen to be free. But don't use your freedom as an excuse to live in sin. Instead, serve one another in love." (Galatians 5:13 NIRV)

✓ EPHESIANS: Christ is the powerful head of the church.

"God placed all things under Christ's rule. He appointed him to be ruler over everything for the church." (Ephesians 1:22 NIRV)

✓ PHILIPPIANS: Christ is the supplier of every need.

"And my God will supply your every need according to His glorious riches in Christ Jesus." (Philippians 4:19 NET)

✓ COLOSSIANS: Christ is Lord over everything.

"For in him all things were created: things in heaven and on earth, visible and invisible, whether thrones or powers or rulers or authorities; all things have been created through him and for him." (Colossians 1:16 NIV)

✓ 1 & 2 THESSALONIANS: Christ is our returning Lord.

"For the Lord himself will come down from heaven, with a loud command, with the voice of the archangel and with the trumpet call of God, and the dead in Christ will rise first. After that, we who are still alive and are left will be caught up together with them in the clouds to meet the Lord in the air. And so we will be with the Lord forever." (1 Thessalonians 4:16-17 NIV)

✓ 1 TIMOTHY: Christ is our mediator.

"For there is one God and one mediator between God and mankind, the man Christ Jesus..." (1 Timothy 2:5 NIV)

✓ 2 TIMOTHY: Christ is the giver of crowns.

"Now there is in store for me the crown of righteousness, which the Lord, the righteous Judge, will award to me on that day—and not only to me, but also to all who have longed for his appearing." (2 Timothy 4:8 NIV)

✓ TITUS: Christ is our blessed hope.

"That's how we should live as we wait for the blessed hope God has given us. We are waiting for Jesus Christ to appear in all his glory. He is our great God and Savior." (Titus 2:13 NIRV)

✓ PHILEMON: Christ is the renewer of hearts.

"Renew my heart. We know that Christ is the one who really renews it." (Philemon 20b NIRV)

Experience God's grace overflowing to your life every day because you are in Christ, who is the answer to your every spiritual need. With joy, live dependently on Him.

Enjoy!

Paul and His Letters

GRACE OVERFLOWING 1

"Paul, a servant of Christ Jesus, called to be an apostle and set apart for the gospel of God...To all in Rome who are loved by God and called to be his holy people: Grace and peace to you from God our Father and from the Lord Jesus Christ. (Romans 1:1, 7 NIV)

CHRIST IS EVERYTHING WE NEED

If you want to say hello to a friend who lives far away, what methods would you likely use today?

You probably mentioned texting, Facebook, email, and/or phone call. Those are great ways to instantly communicate to someone you know and love. Fifty years ago, the only ways to talk to someone who lived far away was by phone call using a phone attached to the wall and by writing letters or sending a telegram. But, 150 years before that, letters were the only method you could use, knowing that your friend wouldn't receive your letter for a week, maybe a month or more. How would you like that?

In the New Testament of our Bible are 13 letters written by a man named Paul. Once you know some of Paul's story, then you'll see why he wrote so many letters.

Paul was a real person who lived at the same time as Jesus and for many years afterwards. We have no indication that he had ever met Jesus before the Resurrection. Paul was a very well-educated and devout Jew. At first, he didn't believe Jesus was the Son of God and fought against Christians, dragging them out of their homes and putting them in prison. Paul made it his mission to get rid of this group of believers in Jesus as the Messiah. The first Christians were known as "those belonging to the Way." One day, while traveling from

Jerusalem to Damascus (in Syria), Jesus confronted him about this misdirected "mission."

Read Acts 9:1-14.

What happened to Paul while he was traveling?

What did Jesus say to Paul?

After that, what did Paul do for the next three days?

Paul believed the vision and changed from being an enemy who hated Jesus into a friend who loved Jesus. Right away, Jesus gave him a specific job to do.

Read Acts 9:15.

What specific job did Jesus give to Paul? [Note: The Gentiles were all non-Jewish people.]

Several years after Paul trusted in Jesus as His Savior, he moved up to **Antioch** to pastor the church there with his friend Barnabas. While a group of church leaders was praying, the Holy Spirit told them to send Paul and Barnabas to faraway places to tell people about Jesus. Today, we would call Paul and Barnabas "missionaries."

Paul made three different "Missionary Journeys" from Antioch to many different cities in the Roman Empire. As a young man, he was known by his Hebrew name "Saul." But, as he traveled throughout the Roman Empire among non-Jewish people, he most often used his Roman name "Paul."

In each city that Paul and his co-workers visited, people heard Paul's message about Jesus and became Christians. They met together and formed a church in that city. Paul loved those people very much and wanted to hear how the young churches were doing. Someone would bring him news about the church members in a particular city then Paul would write them a letter, usually answering some questions they had or teaching them something they needed to know about living as Christians.

The Holy Spirit guided Paul to write those letters and preserved 13 of them for us to have in our Bibles. In fact, Paul authored more of the New Testament writings than anyone else. These letters are a gift to us 2000 years later.

THE JOURNEYS

Follow these brief overviews of Paul's missionary journeys, including some highlights or important diversions. You can follow their journeys on the map provided.

First journey:

Paul and Barnabas started at Antioch and traveled by boat to Cyprus. A few months later, they traveled by boat then lots of walking to towns in the area of Galatia—Psidian Antioch, Iconium, Lystra, Derbe. Most of these people weren't Jewish and worshipped other gods before believing in Jesus.

Paul and Barnabas returned to Antioch where Paul wrote *Galatians*, the first letter to a church.

Second journey:

After some time in Antioch, Paul wanted to go back and visit his Galatian friends. He and his new partner Silas walked back to Derbe and Lystra where a teenager named Timothy joined the travelers. Paul wanted to visit other cities in that area, but the Holy Spirit sent him to Troas (along the west coast). At Troas, God gave Paul a dream about

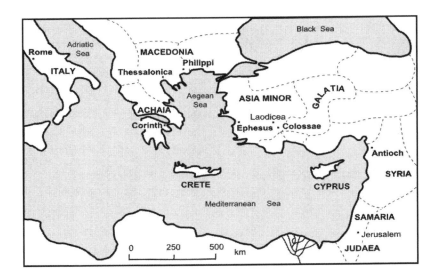

a man from Macedonia (northern Greece) saying, "Come over and help us."

Paul obeyed the vision and sailed with his friends across the sea then walked to Philippi. They spent a few weeks in Philippi and 3 weeks in nearby Thessalonica. Paul went from there to Athens and then to Corinth where he spent two years and wrote *First & Second Thessalonians* before returning home to Antioch.

Third journey:

Back in Antioch, Paul wanted to go visiting again. He traveled through Galatia then to Ephesus where he stayed for 3 years. Then, he went to Thessalonica, Corinth, and back to Ephesus. Paul wrote *First & Second Corinthians* and the letter to the *Romans* during his third missionary journey. Paul ended this journey in Jerusalem to deliver some money that the Greek churches sent to help the poverty-stricken Jewish Christians in Jerusalem and Judea. Paul was arrested in Jerusalem.

First imprisonment:

From Jerusalem, Paul was transferred to Caesarea where he spent two years in confinement. When he appealed to Caesar to hear his case, he was transferred by boat to Rome for another 2 years of house arrest. While in Rome, Paul wrote *Ephesians, Philippians, Colossians,* and *Philemon.*

Fourth journey time:

After Paul's release from house arrest in Rome, he traveled with Timothy to Ephesus where he left Timothy to pastor the church there. Paul traveled with Titus to Crete and established churches there, leaving Titus as pastor. While Paul traveled back in the area of Macedonia, he wrote *First Timothy* and *Titus* to encourage and instruct the young pastors.

Second imprisonment:

Paul was arrested again and placed in a Roman dungeon where he wrote his last letter, *Second Timothy.* Paul was executed shortly thereafter (~67 AD).

THE LETTERS

Find all thirteen letters in your print or digital Bible's Table of Contents, beginning with Romans and ending with Philemon.

Years after Paul wrote his letters, these 13 were collected and organized in the New Testament by size and type. The first nine in the list were written to churches (Romans, 1 and 2 Corinthians, Galatians, Ephesians, Philippians, Colossians, 1 and 2 Thessalonians). The last 4 letters were written to individual people (1 and 2 Timothy, Titus and Philemon).

When we write a letter, we usually start it by saying "Dear friend" or Hello there." At the end, we sign our names. Paul both greets the people and signs his name at the beginning of each letter.

> *In the verses below, look for the words Paul uses to identify himself. Notice the two words—grace and peace—that he uses in each one to greet the recipients.*

- Romans 1:1,7—

- 1st Corinthians 1:1,3—

- 2nd Corinthians 1:1-2—

- Galatians 1:1-3—

- Ephesians 1:1-2—

- Philippians 1:1-2—

- Colossians 1:1-2—

- 1 Thessalonians 1:1—

- 2 Thessalonians 1:1-2—

- 1 Timothy 1:1-2—

- 2 Timothy 1:1-2—

- Titus 1:1,4—

- Philemon 1-3—

Paul identifies himself in several ways—as an apostle, a messenger sent by God, and a bondservant of Jesus Christ. In each of Paul's greetings, you read the same two words: *grace* and *peace*.

Grace means "undeserved favor." The Gentiles wished each other favor with the gods they worshiped so grace was a familiar word for them. Paul taught that Jesus' death on the cross is God's grace gift (His favor) who takes away our sin (wrong things we think and do). God gives us His grace every day so we have strength to live to please Him. Praise God for His grace overflowing to you!

The Jews wished each other "peace" (shalom). So peace was a familiar word for them. Paul taught that Jesus gives us peace with God by making us God's friends because our sins are forgiven. Nothing can ever take our relationship with God away from us. This helps us to feel peaceful and blessed by God instead of worried about the eternal future. Praise God for His peace given to you!

Paul used both words in each letter to reach out to both the Jewish and Gentile Christians in the churches and to bring the two groups together in their common faith.

We have the same kinds of problems in our lives today as they did back then, and Christ is still the answer to our problems as well!

Through these lessons, you will become familiar with the people receiving each letter, the challenges they were facing (needs similar to your own), and the biblical solutions God gave to them (and us) through Paul.

Paul presents Jesus Christ as the answer to their need. We'll see that we have the same kinds of problems in our lives today and that Christ is still the answer to our problems as well through His overflowing grace.

With each letter, you will learn a phrase describing how Christ is presented in that letter as the answer to a particular need.

Read Philippians 1:21.

What does Paul declare about his life?

"To live is Christ" is how Paul described his own life. Jesus, God's son who gave his life on the cross for our sins, is also known as Christ. Christ is the title for the one God promised to come and save the world.

He is both savior and king of planet Earth. In many places in the New Testament, He is also called the Lord Jesus Christ.

Read 1 Timothy 1:12-16.

Rewrite verses 13-14, inserting your name and what characteristics defined your life before Christ.

Why did God show mercy to Paul and to you?

Paul's life was changed from the inside out. He became a beacon of Christ's life shining through his own life. Christ displayed Himself through Paul's life because grace overflowed into his life. Paul understood God's grace so well because he desperately needed it for life. He firmly believed this truth: **Christ is everything we need** for life.

Christ is everything you need for life. He is the answer to your specific needs and meets these needs in your life as you trust in Him to do it. Your life will also be changed from the inside out.

Christ's life will shine through your life as you learn to live dependently on Him and His grace overflowing to your life.

LIVING DEPENDENTLY ON CHRIST

1) Bible verse to learn:

"Paul, a servant of Christ Jesus, called to be an apostle and set apart for the gospel of God...To all in Rome who are loved by God and called to be his holy people: Grace and peace to you from God our Father and from the Lord Jesus Christ. (Romans 1:1, 7)

2) Response in prayer & praise:

What are your biggest challenges in life? Ask Jesus to show you through these lessons how He is the answer to each one of those needs.

3) Getting to know Him more:

Spend a few minutes each day reading these passages and reflecting on how God's marvelous grace offers you a life of freedom and joy. This week you will be reading Acts chapters 9-15 to get a historical perspective on Paul's life and writings.

Read Acts chapter 9.

Reflect on what you read.

Read Acts chapter 10.

Reflect on what you read.

Read Acts chapter 11.

Reflect on what you read.

Read Acts chapter 12.

Reflect on what you read.

Read Acts chapter 13.

Reflect on what you read.

Read Acts chapter 14.

Reflect on what you read.

Read Acts chapter 15.

Reflect on what you read.

The Letter to the Romans

*"This **righteousness** from God comes through faith in Jesus Christ to all who believe." (Romans 3:22 NIV)*

THE KEY QUESTION

While growing up, were you better at playing a sport than your brother or sister was? Or, were you better at making good grades in school or more talented than a sibling? Did that make your parents love you more than them? If you were not as good at sports or grades, did they love you less? Hopefully, your answer is "no." Good parents who truly love their children do so equally regardless of one's ability or achievement. And, they take into account what each child needs and how their differences are expressed. Good parents can give equal love to their children while allowing them to do different things.

The key word for our lesson today is **equal**. The question to ask is: "How are we equal?" Some of Paul's friends needed to know how they could be equal to other people in God's eyes while still being different.

THE PEOPLE AND THEIR NEED

Today's letter was written to a group of believers living in **Rome**, the largest city in the Roman Empire. The Romans were hardworking, highly organized people who built towns and roads throughout the Roman Empire. They were proud of their accomplishments, and Rome was the center of their world.

We do not know who started the church at Rome. After Jesus' resurrection, Roman Jews visiting Jerusalem for Passover heard Peter preach the gospel in Acts 2:10 ("some visitors from Rome") and believed. They may have gone back to Rome, shared the gospel with their friends, and started a church of Romans who believed. About 15 years later, Emperor Claudius got mad at the Jews and kicked them out of Rome. For their own safety, Christian Jews left town. At that time, Christianity was still considered part of the Jewish religion. That left mostly Gentiles (non-Jews) in the Roman church. They got used to

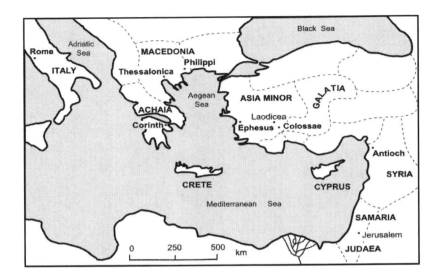

not having the Jewish Christians around and might have even felt relieved not to have them.

The Jewish Christians had a tendency to think they were more righteous (better at worshipping God) than the Gentiles because the Bible was written by Jews and for Jews. Jesus was a Jew, and God had called the Jews His chosen people. After 5 years, it was safe for the Jews to come back to Rome. Suddenly, in the Roman church there were Jewish Christians again who still thought they were better than those who stayed behind. It was not a healthy situation.

While in **Corinth** (see on map) on his 3rd missionary journey, Paul heard what was going on with the Roman church. Though Paul was a Roman citizen, he had not yet been to Rome. He did, however, know quite a few of the Roman Christians and was planning to visit them. The two groups needed to get along. So, he wrote a letter. We have that letter called "Romans." It is a gift from God to us.

In his letter, Paul reminded both groups of Christians—those who had once been Jews and those from non-Jewish backgrounds—that they were **equal** before God. Neither was better than the other. Both had been equally guilty of sin.

By faith in Christ, both had been made equally right with God. Even today, Christ makes us all—from different countries and traditions— equally right and acceptable to God by our faith in Christ. Let's find out what that means.

THE ANSWER: CHRIST IS OUR RIGHTEOUSNESS

In Romans chapters 1, 2 and the first part of three, Paul writes that every person who has ever lived has sinned (done wrong things that displease God). Only Jesus never sinned.

Read Romans 3:9-12.

Who is right with God (righteous) on their own or does anything good in God's eyes on their own?

The phrase "to be right with God" means the same as the word "righteous." When you are right with God or "righteous," you are not separated from Him because of your sin. No one is right with God (righteous) or does anything good in God's eyes on her own. That includes Jews as well as non-Jews.

Read Romans 3:19-20.

"The Law" refers to the rules the Jewish people followed to please God. Will following all the Jewish rules make anyone right with God?

Trying to follow rules makes us aware of what?

Read Romans 3:21-24.

Read the verses one at a time and note what each one says:

- Verse 21—

- Verse 22—

- Verse 23—

- Verse 24—

Jesus Christ, who is completely righteous because He never sinned, died for our sin on the cross. When we believe, He takes our sin away and gives us His righteousness. This makes us acceptable to God. "Justify/justified" means to be declared not guilty of sin. This works equally for every person. In Romans, Christ is our righteousness as described in Romans 3:22.

"This righteousness from God comes through faith in Jesus Christ to all who believe." Romans 3:22

How do we get right with God—by following rules or by faith in Christ?

How do we get right with God—by our own traditions & way of doing things or by faith in Christ?

Christ is our righteousness. That's how everyone's Christian life begins.

So, if you put your trust in Christ to take away your sin, are you more or less right with God than...

- Someone from China who is the top athlete in the world and is also a Christian?
- Someone from Iraq who once worshiped the Muslim god but now worships Jesus?

- Someone from central Africa who once worshiped the sun and moon?
- Someone in professional ministry like Beth Moore, Jennie Allen, or Ann Voscamp?

The answer to the above questions is "neither." Every believer is **equally** right with God and has **equal** righteousness from God. There is no distinction.

Are you confident that you can trust Him and His love for you to be equal to His love for the most famous Christian you know?

In Paul's letter to the Romans, **Christ is our righteousness.** Once you are made right with God by faith in Christ, you receive Christ's righteousness so that when God looks on you, He sees Christ in you. This is God's grace-gift overflowing to you.

God loves all believers equally—regardless of your looks, your career, your family, or your talents. His love for you is perfect.

LIVING DEPENDENTLY ON CHRIST

1) **Bible verse to learn:**

   "This righteousness from God comes through faith in Jesus Christ to all who believe." (Romans 3:22)

2) **Response in prayer & praise:**

   Thank God for His free gift of Jesus. Thank God for sending His Holy Spirit to live in you to help you live a life that pleases your God.

   Thank Jesus for being your righteousness, making you right with God by faith so that you are loved equally by your God.

3) Getting to know Him more:

Spend a few minutes each day reading parts of this wonderful letter and reflecting on how God's marvelous grace offers you a life of freedom and joy.

Read Romans chapter 8.

Reflect on what you read.

Read Romans chapter 12.

Reflect on what you read.

Read Romans chapter 13.

Reflect on what you read.

Read Romans chapter 14.

Reflect on what you read.

Read Romans chapter 15.

Reflect on what you read.

The First Corinthians Letter

*"but to those whom God has called, both Jews and Greeks, Christ the power of God and the **wisdom** of God." (1 Corinthians 1:24 NIV)*

GRACE OVERFLOWING

✓ In ROMANS, **Christ is our righteousness.** Every believer is **equally** right with God and has **equal** righteousness from God.

THE KEY QUESTION

Are people only considered smart if they did very well in school making top grades, or can they be considered smart in other ways? Do you know some really smart people who make bad decisions about how to behave, how to choose friends, or how to treat other people? When we learn information from books, we gain knowledge about the world around us.

When we take knowledge we have learned and make good decisions about how to use that in our lives, we gain what is called **wisdom**. Wisdom is applying what you know to make good decisions for your life.

The key word for our lesson today is **wisdom**. The question to ask is, "Where do we get wisdom?" Some of Paul's friends needed to know the answer to that question.

THE PEOPLE AND THEIR NEED

On his second missionary journey, Paul spent a lot of time in **Corinth,** a big city in southern Greece (see on map). At least 500,000 **Corinthians** lived there. Many of them were very wealthy and thought they were smart because their businesses prospered so much. The Corinthians were Greeks who thought their Greek writings and philosophy were the best in the world—the wisest stuff. They loved listening to traveling teachers and great thinkers so they could learn

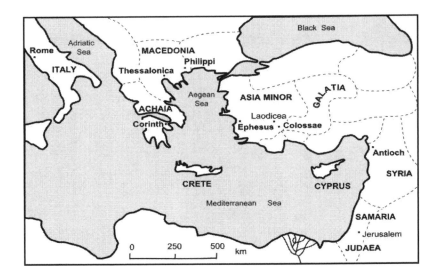

the latest ideas. They thought that their great education could save them. Oh, they could talk Greek philosophy that made them sound very smart. But, they weren't very smart in how they behaved. The Corinthians worshiped idols and were an immoral people, doing some very bad things and not caring who got hurt in the process.

Paul spent about 18 months teaching in Corinth, but not discussing philosophy like the other traveling teachers. Paul taught them that believing God's plan for Jesus to die on the cross and to be raised to life again was true wisdom and the way to be saved. Many Corinthians believed and started a church there.

Read Acts 18:1-17.

Describe some of Paul's experiences in Corinth.

A couple of years later while Paul was in Ephesus (see on map) on his third missionary journey, he learned that the Corinthians were having some problems living as God's people. They were fighting with each other and were bragging about how much knowledge they had. They were just not behaving as they should. So Paul wrote them a letter, discussing the truth about wisdom.

We have that letter called *First Corinthians*. It is a gift of God to us. Paul reminded them (and us) that God's wisdom was better than human education, and Christ is the wisdom of God. Look to Him to find out how to live the best kind of life. Let's see what Paul said.

THE ANSWER: CHRIST IS THE WISDOM OF GOD

Read 1 Corinthians 2:1-5.

What was the focus of Paul's preaching to the Corinthians? [NOTE: verse 3 is a common phrase describing humility.]

What reason did he give for not using the cleverest words to influence them (verse 5)?

In our world, we can be impressed with our own ideas. The Greeks were also impressed with their own ideas. But, God wisely planned that the world would not know Him through its own ideas or its own wisdom (Romans 1:20). It's not education that separates someone from God. Sin separates humans from a holy God. We needed something to take away our sin problem so we could have a relationship with God. God's plan was that His Son Jesus would die for our sins, rise again from the dead, and through faith in Him we would have forgiveness & a relationship with God. **Christ is the wisdom of God.** Paul stressed this in chapter 1.

Read 1 Corinthians 1:24-25.

What is wiser than human wisdom?

What is stronger than human strength?

Paul was referring to Jesus' death and resurrection. The Greeks thought that a savior letting himself get killed was a foolish idea and a sign of weakness. Paul wrote a whole chapter (chapter 15) describing how the resurrection of Jesus from the dead was true and absolutely necessary for our faith.

Paul told the Corinthians that God's plan was wiser and stronger than anything they could get from their own learning. Their learning could not make their sin go away. They needed to trust in Jesus who died for their sins and then became alive again by the power of God. In 1 Corinthians, **Christ is the wisdom of God**.

Read 1 Corinthians 1:26.

Of what does Paul remind the Corinthians about themselves and their own situation in life?

Read 1 Corinthians 1:30-31.

What makes us right with God—our faith in Jesus or how smart we are?

Later in his letter (8:1), Paul tells the Corinthians that knowledge can make people proud. Someone who has had a lot of education, who has advanced in her career, or who is very talented can tend to brag about herself.

What should we brag about if we must brag (verse 31)?

Read 1 Corinthians 1:30 again.

What does Christ do for us?

Holiness means set apart from sin. *Redemption* means we are longer under the power of sin. Christ gives us everything we need to live our lives the way that God desires for us. We learn the wisdom of God in the Bible. With this knowledge, we must choose to want God's wisdom and to apply it to our lives.

Remember that our definition of true wisdom is "applying what you know to make good decisions for your life."

True wisdom means taking knowledge we have learned from Christ in the Bible about how to be holy and making good decisions about how to use that in our lives, while trusting in Christ's power to help us do it.

Let's see how this works in one area of our lives—choosing people to follow as friends or leaders.

Read 1 Corinthians 15:33.

What advice is Paul giving?

Hanging out with the wrong people can lead to being influenced to sin by them. The Corinthians had a tendency to follow the wrong kind of leaders.

Who are the people with the most influence on you?

Considering each one, are they being led by Christ's wisdom given to us in the Bible or by the world's ideas of what is right?

Considering each one, do they mostly brag about Christ's work in their lives or themselves and their own effort?

Christ is the wisdom of God, greater than your human wisdom or strength. He will give you the wisdom to make good choices of friends who will not influence you to sin.

Do you have confidence in Christ as the wisdom and power of God?

LIVING DEPENDENTLY ON CHRIST

1) **Bible verse to learn:**

   "but to those whom God has called, both Jews and Greeks, Christ the power of God and the wisdom of God." (1 Corinthians 1:24 NIV)

2) **Response in prayer & praise:**

   Thank God for His wisdom and plan to send Jesus to meet your need for wisdom in your life. Desire to please God with your life and choice of friends or influencers to follow. Ask Jesus to help you do this.

3) **Getting to know Him more:**

Spend a few minutes each day reading parts of this wonderful letter and reflecting on how God's marvelous grace offers you a life of freedom and joy.

Read 1 Corinthians 1.

Reflect on what you read.

Read 1 Corinthians 2.

Reflect on what you read.

Read 1 Corinthians 12.

Reflect on what you read.

Read 1 Corinthians 13.

Reflect on what you read.

Read 1 Corinthians 15.

Reflect on what you read.

The Second Corinthians Letter

*"Praise be to the God and Father of our Lord Jesus Christ, the Father of compassion and the God of all **comfort**, who **comforts** us in all our troubles, so that we can **comfort** those in any trouble with the **comfort** we ourselves receive from God."*
(2 Corinthians 1:3-4 NIV)

GRACE OVERFLOWING

- ✓ In ROMANS, **Christ is our righteousness.** Every believer is **equally** right with God and has **equal** righteousness from God.

- ✓ In 1 CORINTHIANS: **Christ is the wisdom of God**, greater than any human wisdom or strength.

THE KEY QUESTION

What makes you sad? When you are hurting deep inside or having a tough time, what helps you to feel better? Do you feel loved when someone gives you a hug while you are sad? What gives you comfort when you need it the most?

As you might guess, the key word for our lesson today is **comfort**. The question to ask is: "How does Christ give us comfort?" Some of Paul's friends in Corinth needed to understand why God allows hurtful things in the lives of those He loves and how He gives comfort to ease the hurt.

THE PEOPLE AND THEIR NEED

On his second missionary journey, Paul spent a lot of time in the big city of **Corinth** in southern Greece, not far from Athens. From the last lesson, you learned that Greek people were especially interested in listening to traveling teachers so they could learn the latest ideas. As Greeks, the Corinthians loved getting knowledge and discussing ideas. But, they worshiped idols and were a very immoral people, doing some very bad things and not caring who got hurt in the process.

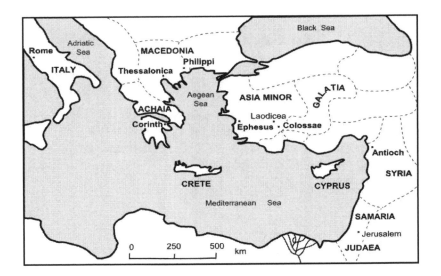

Paul spent a year and a half teaching about Jesus' death and resurrection in Corinth. Quite a few Corinthians believed, and a church was formed.

A couple of years after Paul left Corinth, he heard about some misbehavior in the church there and wrote a letter to them during his third missionary journey to encourage them to do a better job of loving one another.

After Paul wrote that letter called *First Corinthians* (Lesson 3), some bad teachers crept into the church giving the Corinthians very wrong ideas about Jesus and even tried to turn the people against Paul. They said that God must not really be with Paul because Paul was going through some troubles such as getting beaten and thrown in jail. They said that God would never let hurtful things happen to someone He truly loved and who was living the right way.

Paul knew better. So, while he was in **Macedonia** (see on the map), he wrote this letter we call *Second Corinthians* to the people living not only in the city of Corinth but also in the whole surrounding area of Achaia. It is a gift from God to us. In it, Paul says to them and to us that Christians who are loved by God will suffer some troubles in this world, but **Christ is our comforter** when we hurt.

The Answer: Christ Is Our Comforter

Read 2 Corinthians 1:3-5.

What does God do for us when we have trouble and why?

What does it mean to comfort someone or be a comforter for someone?

In 2 Corinthians, **Christ is our comforter.** We share in the comfort Christ gives us when we need it (verse 5). And verse 4 says that Christ comforts us in ALL our troubles. That includes those we cause because of wrong choices we make and those that just seem to happen to us. It also includes those that result from our living out our faith. Paul had experienced the comfort of Christ many times. Let's see what he shares with the Corinthians.

Read 2 Corinthians 1:8-10.

What do you learn about the troubles Paul and his companions experienced?

What did Paul say is the purpose for God letting us go through hurtful times (verse 9)?

God wants us to learn to not depend on ourselves but to depend on God and His great power, which raised Jesus from the dead. He wants us to put our hope in Him and count on His work to deliver us when we are in the midst of troubles.

Read 2 Corinthians 1:11.

What can you do to help someone who is having trouble?

Why will many people give thanks?

Read 2 Corinthians 6:4-7.

What good things did Paul learn through his troubles?

<u>Good character displayed</u>   <u>Difficulties experienced</u>

Who gives us the power to stand firm, to keep doing right, and to continue serving God?

That's a key. None of us can endure troubles without depending on the Spirit's power inside of us to help us get through it without wanting to do the wrong things. Or, even wanting to just quit. It's God's power in us that makes us strong during those times.

Read 2 Corinthians 12:8-10.

Three times, Paul asked for one of his troubles to be taken away. What was God's answer to this man whom God loved dearly?

What was Paul's response to God's decision?

Explain what you think that means and how that might have brought comfort to Paul.

Let's go back to our discussion at the beginning.

Is there anything in your life right now that is very tough, sad, or otherwise painful?

Do you believe that God loves you even though He allows you to go through that pain?

Remember that the best and most loving parents still must let their children hurt sometimes (cutting teeth, riding a bike, gaining and losing friends) in order for them to live as adults. God, who loves you even more than the best parents could every day, wants you to learn how to live as His child, depending on Him for the comfort and strength that flows from God's grace for you.

Human parents raise their children to be less dependent on them and more independent. God raises His children to be less independent and more dependent on Him.

Do you want to do like Paul and depend on God's power to help you do the right thing?

Will you let Christ be your comforter as you endure pain and suffering?

Read John 16:33.

What does Jesus say that His followers will all experience?

Christians who are loved by God will suffer some troubles in this world, but **Christ is our comforter** when we hurt.

Consider those areas of your life where you are needing Christ's comfort right now. Often God uses our Christian brothers and sisters to share Christ's comfort with us.

With whom have you shared your pain?

Have you allowed them to pray for you? To assist you? To give you comfort?

LIVING DEPENDENTLY ON CHRIST

1) Bible verse to learn:

*"Praise be to the God and Father of our Lord Jesus Christ, the Father of compassion and the God of all **comfort**, who **comforts** us in all our troubles, so that we can **comfort** those in any trouble with the **comfort** we ourselves receive from God."*
(2 Corinthians 1:3-4 NIV)

2) Response in prayer & praise:

Turn to Christ for comfort in your pain. Trust in the Holy Spirit's power in you to give you strength to do what is right in the midst of your troubles. Thank God for His faithfulness and kindness to work in your life.

3) Getting to know Him more:

Spend a few minutes each day reading this wonderful letter and reflecting on how God's marvelous grace offers you a life of freedom and joy.

Read 2 Corinthians chapter 4.

Reflect on what you read.

Read 2 Corinthians chapter 5.

Reflect on what you read.

Read 2 Corinthians chapter 6.

Reflect on what you read.

Read 2 Corinthians chapter 11.

Reflect on what you read.

Read 2 Corinthians chapter 12.

Reflect on what you read.

The Letter to the Galatians

*"My brothers and sisters, you were chosen to be free. But don't use your **freedom** as an excuse to live in sin. Instead, serve one another in love." (Galatians 5:13 NIRV)*

GRACE OVERFLOWING

- ✓ In ROMANS, **Christ is our righteousness.** Every believer is equally right with God and has equal righteousness from God.

- ✓ In 1 CORINTHIANS: **Christ is the wisdom of God**, greater than any human wisdom or strength.

- ✓ In 2 CORINTHIANS: **Christ is our comforter** when we hurt.

THE KEY QUESTION

Have you ever taken an art class or even thought about taking an art class? Let's say you have an art teacher who says art begins with a blank sheet of paper and lots of different colors. Then, you can paint whatever your heart desires on the paper. That art teacher moves away. You get a new art teacher who says art should be done on a paper with a big square on it. Men can have 3 paint colors, and women can only have 2 colors. And, you have to keep whatever you paint inside the lines of the square. Would you like that? Which type of painting gives you more freedom and is more enjoyable?

The key word for our lesson today is **freedom**. The question to ask is, "Freedom to do what?" Some of Paul's friends needed to know the answer to that question.

THE PEOPLE AND THEIR NEED

On his first missionary journey, Paul and Barnabas visited four towns in an area called **Galatia** (see the map). It is in the center of modern Turkey. The people who lived there were called **Galatians** and were mostly Greeks and Romans who didn't know God. Some Jews lived there as well. Whenever Paul visited a town, he'd go to the local

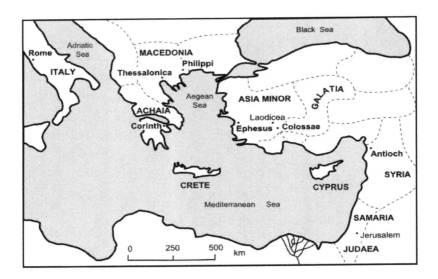

synagogue, which was a small church building. Jews met there to worship God every Saturday like we do at churches in our towns. Greeks and Romans who wanted to worship God joined them there. As a traveling teacher, Paul was invited to speak to everyone at the synagogue meeting. So, he gave them the good news about Jesus.

In each town, a few Jews believed Paul's message about Jesus, but it was mostly the Greeks and Romans who listened to Paul and trusted in Jesus to take away their sins. The new Christians started meeting together with Paul who taught them about Jesus and their new freedom to love and serve God because their sins were totally forgiven. This made the Jewish synagogue leaders jealous because the Greeks and Romans were becoming Christians instead of becoming Jews! So the Jewish leaders chased Paul out of every town. In one town, they tried to kill him by throwing large rocks at him. He was badly hurt, but thankfully he didn't die. Bravely, Paul went back to each town, appointing leaders for the new churches. Then, he and Barnabas headed back to Antioch to report back to the church there and praise God together.

Back in Antioch, Paul heard that another teacher had gone to those Galatian towns and told the new Christians that God's gift of Jesus was not enough to get rid of sin! The bad teacher said they also had to follow "the Law" of Moses in addition to believing in Jesus. Only by following the Law every day could anyone be truly forgiven by God for their sin. For example, you had to eat Jewish food. No ham or shrimp.

You had to wash your dishes by the rules. Following that Law is like having to paint inside the square instead of all over the page. The people had become confused. So Paul wrote them a letter and explained to them the freedom they had in Christ and how not to give up on it.

We have that letter called Galatians. It is a gift from God to us. Paul says to them and to us that in Christ, there is freedom. What kind of freedom? Let's find out.

THE ANSWER: CHRIST IS OUR FREEDOM FROM THE LAW

Read Galatians 2:16.

How do we become right with God and have our sins forgiven—by following a lot of special rules or by faith in Jesus only?

During the time of Moses (as described in the Old Testament books of *Exodus and Leviticus),* God gave the Jewish people many laws for their nation. These laws fit into three categories—religious (mostly for having sins forgiven), civil (how to run the government), and moral (how people should treat one another).

God gave those laws so people would realize how sinful we all are and that we all needed God's mercy and help because no one could ever follow all of them all of the time. On God's "test," anything less than 100% is failing, and only Jesus has ever gotten 100!

God's laws also taught His people what holiness is and how they could live their lives God's way, just like the way a parent or guardian trains a child to become a responsible adult. The Law was just in charge until Christ came, but we are no longer under its control.

"So the law was our guardian until Christ came that we might be justified by faith. Now that this faith has come, we are no longer under a guardian." (Galatians 3:24-25)

Suppose someone said to you, "You know, in order for you to have all your sins forgiven, you MUST attend church every week" or "In order to have all your sins forgiven, you HAVE to take communion every week." How would you answer?

Neither of those activities are bad for you. The point Paul was trying to make to the Galatians. If you've already been given eternal life there's nothing more you need to do, no other rules you must follow just to be saved or to stay saved. And, Paul even says it is "foolish" to believe anything else!

Should you obey others if they tell you to do something that is different from what the Bible says?

In Galatians, **Christ is our freedom from the law**, freedom from having to follow extra rules just to maintain our salvation.

Read Galatians 5:1.

What words did Paul use to describe what the bad teachers had done to the Galatians?

A yoke of slavery refers to chains and bondage. Paul told the Galatian Christians (5:1) that the bad teachers had put chains on them to make them slaves to the Jewish Law. Broken chains would make a good symbol for this freedom that Christ gives all believers.

When the Galatians got this letter, do you think they felt like those chains were now broken so they could be free again?

Read Galatians 5:13-15.

Christ is our **freedom from the law**. Freedom is the key word.

What does verse 13 tell us about our freedom?

In verses 14-15, what should govern our freedom?

Thinking about artwork again. Even if you are given a blank piece of paper and lots of paint colors, you are still not free to do some things. You aren't free to paint the floor or someone else's paper. Those things would affect someone else negatively. In the same way, we are not free to do anything we want with our lives.

God still wants us to love one another, not kill anyone, not lie, not steal, not cheat, and not be hateful. Those rules about how to live are still good for us to follow.

Read Galatians 3:14.

Once we are made right with God who comes to live inside us?

Read Galatians 5:16-21.

What freedom does the Spirit give to us?

The term "flesh" (or "sinful nature") refers to that portion of ourselves through which sin assaults us. We don't know what it is, but we know how it works—sending messages to the mind that are in conflict with the Spirit. The flesh does not improve or change its nature over time as long as we are in our bodies. At the moment of salvation, we are born again of the Spirit. Our bodies are **not** born again, and our souls (mind, emotions, and will) are **not** instantly transformed. While the flesh doesn't improve, our choices can change over time as we learn to live by the Spirit.

There is a story about a little boy who was standing in his chair. His mother told him to sit down. The little boy sat down, but he told his mother that while he was sitting on the outside he was still standing up on the inside. Have you ever felt that way when someone made you do something you didn't want to do, even if it was something good?

Do you think God wants you to be loving and kind to someone because you have to or because you want to do so?

God is more interested in your heart behavior. He wants you to choose to do the right things because your heart wants to do so, especially to love one another.

When is it hard to love someone or be kind to someone?

Who gives us the power to love someone or be kind to someone when it is hard?

The Holy Spirit works from the inside out. He gives us love that comes from our hearts not just because we are told to do so.

We can ask God's Holy Spirit to help us love others, especially when it is hard. The Bible calls that bearing fruit. Let's see what Paul says a person with the Holy Spirit living inside should be like—the kind of spiritual fruit you will bear.

Read Galatians 5:22-23.

What kinds of "fruit" does the Holy Spirit produce?

These are not the only fruit the Holy Spirit produces. But, this fruit in our lives makes our lives more like Jesus' life. Christ is our **freedom from** the law to have our sins forgiven. In Christ, we have **freedom to** love others and bear spiritual fruit from our hearts.

In Galatians, **Christ is our freedom from the law** of works to earn God's acceptance. Salvation is based on faith in Christ alone not by works. Paul's emphasis on freedom expressed in this letter fueled the Protestant Reformation, which helped to bring God's grace and a love for God's Word to millions around the world.

LIVING DEPENDENTLY ON CHRIST

1) **Bible verse to learn:**

   *"My brothers and sisters, you were chosen to be free. But don't use your **freedom** as an excuse to live in sin. Instead, serve one another in love." (Galatians 5:13 NIRV)*

2) **Response in prayer & praise:**

   What is your heart response to this gift of freedom God has given to you in Christ?

Thank God for the gift of His Holy Spirit to lead your heart to do the right things. Ask Jesus to help you be more intentional to love someone or be kind to someone this week when it is hard to do so.

3) **Getting to know Him more:**

Spend a few minutes each day reading this wonderful letter and reflecting on how God's marvelous grace offers you a life of freedom and joy.

Read Galatians chapter 1.

Reflect on what you read.

Read Galatians chapter 2.

Reflect on what you read.

Read Galatians chapter 3.

Reflect on what you read.

Read Galatians chapter 4.

Reflect on what you read.

Read Galatians chapter 5.

Reflect on what you read.

Read Galatians chapter 6.

Reflect on what you read.

The Letter to the Ephesians

*"God placed all things under Christ's **rule**. He appointed him to be **ruler** over everything for the church." (Ephesians 1:22 NIRV)*

GRACE OVERFLOWING

- ✓ In ROMANS, **Christ is our righteousness.** Every believer is equally right with God and has equal righteousness from God.

- ✓ In 1 CORINTHIANS: **Christ is the wisdom of God**, greater than any human wisdom or strength.

- ✓ In 2 CORINTHIANS: **Christ is our comforter** when we hurt.

- ✓ In GALATIANS: **Christ is our freedom from the law** of works to earn God's acceptance.

THE KEY QUESTION

Some people wear things that they think gives them good luck—a pair of socks, a special shirt, a rabbit's foot. What about you? Do you possess anything that you think gives you good luck? Why do you consider that item as lucky? Do you think that item really has power to give you good luck?

Likewise, some things are associated with causing bad luck—walking under a ladder, breaking a mirror, or stepping on the cracks in a sidewalk. But, do you think those things really have power to give you bad luck?

The key word for our lesson today is **power**. The questions to ask are, "What kind of power? What has the greatest power?" Some of Paul's friends needed to know the answer to that question.

THE PEOPLE AND THEIR NEED

On his third missionary journey, Paul spent time in **Ephesus**, a large city of 250,000 people (see the map). The people living there were called **Ephesians** and were obsessed with power, especially witchcraft

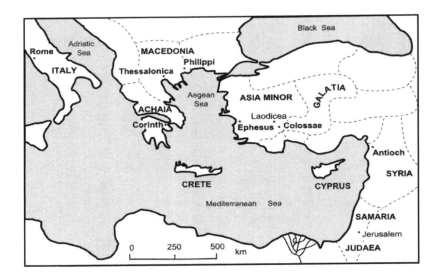

and magic. They were very afraid of evil spirits and bad luck so they clung to anything that would keep them safe—magic words written on socks or recited aloud to chase evil spirits away, necklaces with magic power to give them luck when playing sports, and books of magic spells to keep them safe. Ephesus was a mess!

So, Paul spent three years with the Ephesians, teaching classes every day to those who wanted to learn a new way to live. And, God did "extra-miraculous" miracles through Paul. (You can read about this in Acts 19:8-20.) God showed them that He was **more powerful** than their magicians, lucky charms, and magic words. God was more powerful than the evil spirits or any substitute they might trust for protection against evil. God knew what they really needed—Himself!

Many Ephesians trusted in Jesus for their protection then they got rid of their substitutes. They had a big bonfire to burn their sorcerer's manuals, lucky socks, and magic necklaces. They attended Paul's classes then spread out and shared the good news about Jesus throughout the whole area, establishing churches all over the place. Seven years later, while Paul was a prisoner in Rome, he wrote a letter to the church in Ephesus, and churches in the surrounding area, reminding them that no matter how hard life gets, Jesus Christ is the powerful head of the Church—more powerful than any substitute "lucky charm." Paul tells them that Christ will return someday to rule over earth and defeat all evil. And Paul tells them Christ's power makes it possible for them to live God's way today and not be afraid.

The Holy Spirit guided Paul as he wrote this letter so it is a gift from God to us. Paul says to them and to us: in Christ there is more power than anything else we can trust for good luck. Let's find out how powerful Christ is and how His power works for us.

THE ANSWER: CHRIST IS THE POWERFUL HEAD OF THE CHURCH

Read Ephesians 1:13-14.

When the Ephesians believed the good news, what did God give to them?

Let's see what Paul says about this mighty power of God in us.

Read Ephesians 1:19-23.

In verses 19-20, what does Paul want the Ephesians to know about the might of God's power?

God's power is great. It can't be compared with anything else. No substitutes for good luck are as powerful as God. And, His power is at work for us who believe.

In verses 21-23, what power does Christ have?

In heaven, Christ has the power of a great king—king above all other powers and kings.

Does that mean Christ is ruler over even the evil spirits? Is He ruler over anything that causes bad luck?

What is Christ's role specifically for the body of believers called the Church?

In Ephesians, **Christ is the powerful head of the Church.** He is the ruler, the head who fills every need in every way. The Church includes everyone who has already trusted in Christ for salvation. With Christ ruling over believers and living in believers through His Spirit, there isn't any need for lucky socks, magic words, or special charms to keep bad things from happening to the Ephesians, or to you.

Paul is saying, "Why trust in a substitute power like luck or magic which can never be as powerful as Jesus Christ Himself to help you live a good life?" Jesus' power is available to every believer. Jesus Christ is living inside you through His Holy Spirit. Jesus Christ is the powerful head of the Church.

Read Ephesians 3:16-20.

Paul prayed for the Ephesians (and us!) to know this power working within Christians. What does Christ's power within us help us to know (verse 18)?

What confidence do you get from knowing the truth about how much God loves you?

Is there a limit to Christ's power working within us?

Christ's power works **in us** to help us live God's way and **for us** to protect us from anything evil. Let's look at both of those.

1. CHRIST'S POWER WORKING INSIDE US:

Read the following verses.

What godly behaviors require Christ's power in us?

- Ephesians 4:2—

- Ephesians 4:15—

- Ephesians 4:26—

- Ephesians 4:29—

- Ephesians 4:32—

- Ephesians 5:21—

These godly behaviors are hard to do and do not come naturally to us. Christ's power in us enables us to live God's way as we trust Him to work in and through us. By faith, we can access His power to help us.

2. CHRIST'S POWER WORKING FOR US:

We will have trouble in this world because evil still exists until Christ returns. Paul told the Ephesians and us how to overcome bad things by trusting in the power of Christ to hold onto us and protect us.

Read Ephesians 6:10-11, 13.

Who can make you strong against anything bad happening to you?

What does Christ provide for you to put on?

The armor that Christ provides for you isn't real armor. It's things we KNOW to be true—spiritual armor. Christ gives us this armor so we can stand strong whenever we are attacked or tested. By using this armor, we learn to trust in Christ's power rather than our own.

Helmet of salvation:

A helmet protects the head of the soldier. When we have trusted Jesus Christ as our Savior, He's always with us, ready to protect us no matter what happens! Our salvation comes from Jesus and lasts forever. Remember that you have this helmet when someone makes you doubt that you are saved.

Breastplate of righteousness:

A breastplate protects a soldier's chest and everything inside – the heart, lungs, stomach and liver. Our breastplate of righteousness reminds us that in Christ we are totally forgiven. We are protected from the devil's accusations about our sin because we have been given Jesus' righteousness! Remember you have this breastplate when you've done something wrong and don't feel that God has forgiven you.

Shield of faith:

A shield protects a soldier from arrows and sword attacks. Our faith is in the truth that God always loves us and is always with us. Our shield of faith stops the thoughts that God doesn't love us because we've done something wrong. When we shield ourselves with faith, we can handle anything!

Belt of truth:

The soldier's belt holds his weapons—knife and sword. When you know the truths in God's Word, you'll know how He wants you to live and can make good choices. Just like the belt on your pants keeps them from falling down, the belt of truth keeps you from falling down by making bad choices.

Shoes of the gospel of peace:

Soldiers needed good strong sandals to protect their feet so they could be ready to go wherever they were needed to fight. The Romans kept peace in the Empire so shoes represent our peace with God. We also need to remember our "gospel shoes" and be ready to share Jesus with others so they can have peace with God, too.

Sword of the Spirit:

Soldiers used a short and lightweight sword to attack. The sword of the Spirit is God's Word. It is also the Spirit of God working in us. God's Word cuts to the heart of anyone who hears it. We need to know it well so it can be used easily for ourselves and to share with others.

Prayer:

This isn't really a particular piece of armor but kind of holds all our armor together. By talking to God in fearful situations, we can trust Him to do amazing things on our behalf. Nothing is too big or impossible with prayer because God can do anything that He wants to do. He will answer the way He knows is best.

In Isaiah 59:17, God Himself puts on a breastplate of righteousness and a helmet of salvation to fight battles for His people. Isn't that a comforting picture? With this armor, we are soldiers of the living God and "more than conquerors through Him who loved us" (Romans 8:37).

Trust Jesus' power to protect you and bring good into your life rather than lucky socks, shirts, diplomas or any other thing. Christ is more powerful than any substitute we could trust instead of Him. He is the powerful head of the Church, which includes all believers. You can trust Jesus Christ's power to protect you and bring good into your life rather than anything you might consider substituting for Him.

Christ's power makes it possible for us to live God's way TODAY and not be afraid.

LIVING DEPENDENTLY ON CHRIST

1) Bible verse to learn:

"God placed all things under Christ's rule. He appointed him to be ruler over everything for the church." (Ephesians 1:22 NIRV)

2) Response in prayer & praise:

What things have you been relying upon for power in your life? Are you willing to give up those substitutes and rely on Jesus' power alone to bring success in your spiritual life?

Ask Jesus to help you know how much you are dearly and deeply loved by your God. Then, choose to trust in Christ's power working within you to make a difference in your life.

3) Getting to know Him more:

Spend a few minutes each day reading this wonderful letter and reflecting on how God's marvelous grace offers you a life of freedom and joy.

Read Ephesians chapter 1.

Reflect on what you read.

Read Ephesians chapter 2.

Reflect on what you read.

Read Ephesians chapter 3.

Reflect on what you read.

Read Ephesians chapter 4.

Reflect on what you read.

Read Ephesians chapter 5.

Reflect on what you read.

Read Ephesians chapter 6.

Reflect on what you read.

The Letter to the Philippians

*"And my God will **supply** your every need according to His glorious riches in Christ Jesus." (Philippians 4:19 NET)*

GRACE OVERFLOWING

✓ In ROMANS, **Christ is our righteousness.** Every believer is equally right with God and has equal righteousness from God.

✓ In 1 CORINTHIANS: **Christ is the wisdom of God**, greater than any human wisdom or strength.

✓ In 2 CORINTHIANS: **Christ is our comforter** when we hurt.

✓ In GALATIANS: **Christ is our freedom from the law** of works to earn God's acceptance.

✓ In EPHESIANS: **Christ is the powerful head of the church.** Christ's power works in us to help us live God's way and for us to protect us from anything evil.

THE KEY QUESTION

Do you remember the last thank-you note you received? Who wrote it and why was it written? Recall the last thank-you note you sent. What was the reason?

Now recall a time when you needed something, and God supplied what you needed. Did you say "thank you" to God? Did you thank the person whom God used to supply what you needed?

Everybody needs to write thank-you notes once in a while—from children to Presidents and Kings. And, receiving a thank-you-note can make anyone feel appreciated.

The key word for this lesson is **supply**. The questions to ask are: "How does God supply what we need? How do we say thank-you?" The letter to the Philippians is a thank-you note from Paul to the Philippian church because they supplied Paul with something he needed. Let's see what Paul shared with his friends.

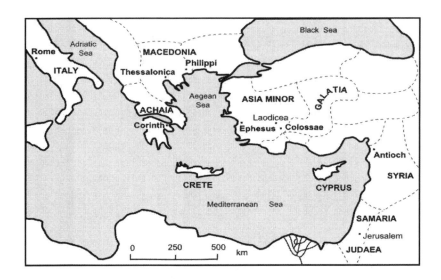

THE PEOPLE AND THEIR NEED

On his second missionary journey while Paul was in Troas (west coast of Turkey), God showed him a vision of a man from Macedonia saying, "Come over and help us." Paul, Silas, Timothy and their new friend Luke (who wrote *Luke* and *Acts*) traveled across the Aegean Sea to **Philippi** (see the map).

At first, Paul shared about Jesus with a group of women (one named Lydia) who worshiped God and met together for prayer. They believed and were joined by many other new believers who responded to Paul's preaching during the weeks he spent in Philippi. Then he and Silas were thrown into prison. That night while they were singing and praising God, an earthquake happened that loosened all the prisoners' chains. But, no one escaped. The prison guard was so grateful that he and his whole family chose to believe in Jesus, too. The new community of Philippian believers met in Lydia's house. You can read about his time there in Acts 16.

Paul was forced to leave Philippi. Yet, the church continued to show their love for him. The Philippians sent money often to supply Paul's needs as a missionary. After his third missionary journey, Paul went to Jerusalem where he was arrested and sent to **Rome** as a prisoner. While there, the Philippians sent one of their own people to encourage Paul and money to supply his needs even though they were very poor.

So, Paul wrote them a letter, thanking them for their gift (among other beautiful things written in it about Christ).

We have that letter called *Philippians*. It is a gift from God to us. Paul says to them and to us that **Christ is the supplier of our needs**. Let's see what he means.

THE ANSWER: CHRIST IS THE SUPPLIER OF EVERY NEED

Read Philippians 1:3-8.

What did Paul say about the Philippians?

How did he feel about them?

Read Philippians 2:25-30.

Whom did the Philippians send to help Paul?

What other information is given about Epaphroditus?

Besides money, Epaphroditus likely brought news about the church as well as hands and feet to help Paul in his imprisonment. He may have also brought encouraging words to Paul. Paul appreciated what the Philippians did.

Read Philippians 4:14-19.

For each of the verses, discover why the Philippians were so dear to Paul.

- Verses 14—

- Verse 15—

- Verse 16—

- Verses 17-18—

According to verse 19, what does God do?

In Philippians, **Christ is the supplier of every need.** And, Christ often supplies the needs for one person through the generosity of another as God has supplied their needs. That's what He did for Paul through the Philippians.

And, Christ was supplying the Philippians' needs so they could help Paul. All was given with love. Needs can be things other than money such as food, help, and encouragement. So you can see why I called this letter a "thank-you" letter from Paul to the Philippians.

Going back to what we discussed at the beginning, what are some ways that friends have been there for you when you really needed help?

How do you feel when you need help and someone helps you?

Philippians 1:4-5 in the NIV says this, "In all my prayers for all of you, I always pray with joy because of your **partnership** in the gospel from the first day until now."

Consider examples in life when people need to have a partner.

Your examples may have included marriage, business, ice-skating, tennis, musical partners in duets, or classroom projects. Partners work together for a common goal—skating partners work together to win a competition, business partners work together to produce a successful product, tennis partners work together to win matches, music partners work together to play concerts, and classroom partners work together to get a good grade.

Paul said he and the church at Philippi were partners. What was their common goal (verse 5)?

With your money, time and talents, you may partner with your local church, a local mission agency, and/or a missionary for the purpose of spreading the gospel, making disciples, and growing God's kingdom on the earth.

And, **Christ is the supplier of every need** of yours so that you can help others.

Living Dependently on Christ

1) Bible verse to learn:

"And my God will supply your every need according to His glorious riches in Christ Jesus." (Philippians 4:19 NET)

2) Response in prayer & praise:

Is there someone in your life who needs help today? Ask Jesus to show you how you can supply a need for them today in His name. Thank God for supplying your needs so you can help others.

3) Getting to know Him more:

Spend a few minutes each day reading this wonderful letter and reflecting on how God's marvelous grace offers you a life of freedom and joy.

Read Philippians chapter 1.

Reflect on what you read.

Read Philippians chapter 2.

Reflect on what you read.

Read Philippians chapter 3.

Reflect on what you read.

Read Philippians chapter 4.

Reflect on what you read.

GRACE OVERFLOWING 8 — The Letter to the Colossians

"For in him all things were created: things in heaven and on earth, visible and invisible, whether thrones or powers or rulers or authorities; all things have been created through him and for him." (Colossians 1:16 NIV)

GRACE OVERFLOWING

- ✓ In ROMANS, **Christ is our righteousness.** Every believer is equally right with God and has equal righteousness from God.

- ✓ In 1 CORINTHIANS: **Christ is the wisdom of God**, greater than any human wisdom or strength.

- ✓ In 2 CORINTHIANS: **Christ is our comforter** when we hurt.

- ✓ In GALATIANS: **Christ is our freedom from the law** of works to earn God's acceptance.

- ✓ In EPHESIANS: **Christ is the powerful head of the church.** Christ's power works **in us** to help us live God's way and **for us** to protect us from anything evil.

- ✓ In PHILIPPIANS: **Christ is the supplier of every need** of yours so that you can help others.

THE KEY QUESTION

What comes to mind when you hear or read the word "lord?" Do you tend to submit to authority or push against it to follow your own way? Many of us like the idea of authority managing everyone and everything else as long as we can keep doing what we like with no one bothering us. Go ahead and admit it. ☺

The key word for our lesson today is **lord**. The questions to ask are, "Who is really 'lord' of our lives, and what does that mean?" Some of Paul's friends needed to know the answer to those questions.

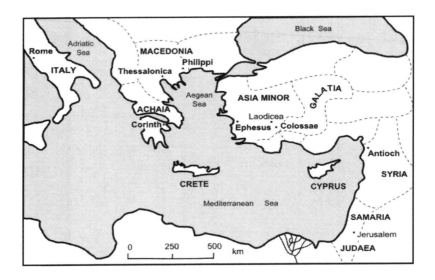

THE PEOPLE AND THEIR NEED

On his third missionary journey, Paul spent 3 years in Ephesus, a large city of at least 250,000 people. While there, Paul held classes every day for anyone wanting to learn about Jesus Christ, having their sins forgiven, and gaining a new way to live. One of Paul's students named Epaphras traveled to the nearby town of **Colossae** (see the map) to teach the Colossians living there. The people were mostly Greeks and Romans who didn't know God. So, Epaphras taught the Colossians the "good news" about Jesus dying for their sins and becoming alive again so that they could believe in Him and receive eternal life.

A few Jews believed the message about Jesus, but it was mostly the Greeks and Romans who listened and trusted in Jesus to take away their sins. They started worshiping God together and learning more about Jesus and their new life as Christians. After Epaphras left Colossae, other men told the new Christians that Epaphras didn't tell them the whole story. Some said that Jesus was not really God, that it's better to worship angels who were closer to God than Jesus was. Others taught that only by following special rules can anyone have a right standing with God. Those rules said you could only eat certain foods, could enjoy nothing fun, and couldn't get married. Yet, none of those rules taught them how to get rid of bad behavior like telling lies, speaking mean words, and getting angry. Seven years after the church was started, Epaphras was so concerned that he traveled to Rome where Paul was a prisoner and told him all about it.

Paul had never met the Colossians, but he loved these young Christians very much. So, Paul wrote a letter that Epaphras carried back to Colossae. Paul knew that Epaphras had taught the Colossians that Jesus Christ was Lord over everything, including angels. Remember that *Jesus* is His name; *Christ* is His title, which refers to His authority as Lord.

In his letter, Paul emphasized the truth that Jesus is Lord over everything. We have that letter called *Colossians*. It is a gift from God to us. Paul says to them and to us that Christ is Lord over everything—angels, creation and even our behavior. What does that look like? Let's find out.

THE ANSWER: CHRIST IS LORD OVER EVERYTHING

Read Colossians 1:15-18.

What does Paul emphasize about Christ in these verses?

- Verse 15—

- Verse 16—

- Verse 17—

- Verse 18—

As God, Christ is the Lord over creation ("firstborn" refers to priority in inheritance). All things were created by and for Him. Jesus Christ is Lord over all creation, including angels. Christ was present before the world was created.

He holds everything together. This might mean that He makes it keep working in the way He planned. Christ is Lord over our world. Jesus died and then became alive again. And, Christ is Lord over the Church, which includes all believers.

In Colossians, **Christ is Lord over everything.** Paul told the Colossian Christians they had received the full story about Jesus from Epaphras. Christ is completely God and as God, He is Lord over everything, including angels. Paul was telling them to not worship angels. Then, he goes on to remind them of something wonderful.

Read Colossians 1:13-14.

What is true about every Christian?

Read Colossians 2:13.

What is true about every Christian?

When we each trust Christ, all of our sins are forgiven. We now can serve God completely with our lives and honor Christ as Lord over our behavior. That's what Paul taught the Colossians as well.

Read Colossians 3:8-9.

What kind of behavior is not appropriate for a follower of Christ who has been given a new life?

Christ as Lord over our behavior wants us to stop our destructive anger, rage, hate, lies, and filthy/mean words. Let's see what kind of behavior is right for us.

Read Colossians 3:12-15, 17, 23.

According to each verse, what kind of behavior is appropriate for a follower of Christ who has been given a new life?

- Verse 12—

- Verse 13—

- Verse 14—

- Verse 15—

- Verse 17—

- Verse 23—

These are hard to do and do not come naturally to us. Paul writes in Colossians 1:29, "To this end I strenuously contend with all the energy Christ so powerfully works in me." Christ's power in us enables us to live this way as we trust Him to work in and through us.

According to verse 15 above, Christ gives you peace in your heart. You are to let that rule your actions like an umpire saying to anger, "You're out!" and to kindness, "You're safe!" Christ is Lord over your behavior.

In verse 17, we are reminded to do everything we say or do in light of Jesus as Lord. We read in verse 23, "Work at everything you do with all your heart. Work as if you were working for the Lord, not for human masters." This applies to any work you do—inside and outside the place where you live.

In Colossians, **Christ is Lord over everything.** He is Lord over the universe, the earth, the angels, and our behavior. As Lord over our behavior, He is powerful enough to change our bad behavior into good behavior that pleases Him. We must choose to submit to Him as Lord. He deserves it!

Our willingness to let Him change us is worshiping Him as Lord.

LIVING DEPENDENTLY ON CHRIST

1) Bible verse to learn:

"For in him all things were created: things in heaven and on earth, visible and invisible, whether thrones or powers or rulers or authorities; all things have been created through him and for him." (Colossians 1:16 NIV)

2) Response in prayer & praise:

Read Psalm 139:23-24. What does David ask of God? Okay, now you pray those verses as a prayer to Jesus.

You are asking Jesus to help you recognize the areas of your life where you are not submitting to Him as Lord. What has He revealed to you? Thank Him for showing it to you and for His forgiveness. Ask Him to make the change in your life so your behavior matches who you are as a follower of Christ.

3) Getting to know Him more:

Spend a few minutes each day reading this wonderful letter and reflecting on how God's marvelous grace offers you a life of freedom and joy.

Read Colossians chapter 1.

Reflect on what you read.

Read Colossians chapter 2.

Reflect on what you read.

Read Colossians chapter 3.

Reflect on what you read.

Read Colossians chapter 4.

Reflect on what you read.

The First and Second Letters to the Thessalonians

9

*"For the Lord himself **will come down from heaven**, with a loud command, with the voice of the archangel and with the trumpet call of God, and the dead in Christ will rise first. After that, we who are still alive and are left will be caught up together with them in the clouds to meet the Lord in the air. And so we will be with the Lord forever." (1 Thessalonians 4:16-17 NIV)*

GRACE OVERFLOWING

- ✓ In ROMANS, **Christ is our righteousness.** Every believer is equally right with God and has equal righteousness from God.

- ✓ In 1 CORINTHIANS: **Christ is the wisdom of God**, greater than any human wisdom or strength.

- ✓ In 2 CORINTHIANS: **Christ is our comforter** when we hurt.

- ✓ In GALATIANS: **Christ is our freedom from the law** of works to earn God's acceptance.

- ✓ In EPHESIANS: **Christ is the powerful head of the church.** Christ's power works **in us** to help us live God's way and **for us** to protect us from anything evil.

- ✓ In PHILIPPIANS: **Christ is the supplier of every need** of yours so that you can help others.

- ✓ In COLOSSIANS: **Christ is Lord over everything.** He is Lord over the universe, the earth, the angels, and our behavior.

THE KEY QUESTION

Do you have siblings or other relatives who live far away? Do you want them to come and visit you? What kinds of things do you do to prepare for guests coming? How do you greet them when they walk in the door? After your guests leave, are you eager for their returning back to visit you again?

Consider babies who are born during a time of war when their fathers are soldiers deployed overseas. The babies may not get to see their dads for months or even a year or more. They may hear about their dads and even see a picture or video feed of them. But, they don't really get to experience knowing their dads until the soldiers return back home. Then, father and child meet face-to-face in a warm embrace of love.

The key word for our lesson today is **returning**. The questions to ask are, "Who is returning, and how do we prepare for it?" Some of Paul's friends needed to know the answer to those questions.

THE PEOPLE AND THEIR NEED

On his second missionary journey while Paul was in Troas (above Ephesus on the map), God showed him a vision of a man from Macedonia saying, "Come over and help us." Paul and Silas went, stopping first at Philippi, where they preached, and a church was formed. After spending a night in prison for driving an evil spirit from a girl, Paul and Silas were forced to leave Philippi. They went down the road to **Thessalonica** (see on map), the capital of Macedonia and a large city of 200,000 people who were called **Thessalonians.** You can read about his time there in Acts 17:1-15.

Paul preached the good news about Jesus' death and resurrection for several weeks in the synagogue in Thessalonica. Some Jews believed as well as a large number of non-Jews. The Jews who didn't believe

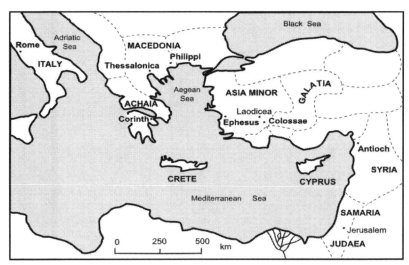

started a riot in the city in order to stop Paul. They rushed to the house where Paul was staying and dragged the owner of the house out of the house to the courthouse. The man was released, but the new Thessalonian believers thought it was too dangerous for Paul to stay so they helped him to escape in the middle of the night.

After he left Thessalonica, Paul went down the road to Berea then to Athens. There he sent his friend Timothy back to Thessalonica to check on the church there. Timothy brought back a good report. In fact, their faith in Christ had become known throughout all of Macedonia. Everyone knew that they had turned away from statues of gods to serve the living and true God. And, they were waiting for Jesus to return from heaven to rescue them from their present hardships. You see, the men who started the riot were making life hard for these new believers, causing much suffering for them.

So, when Paul got to **Corinth** he wrote a letter to them to encourage them during their hardships and to answer their questions about Jesus' return. Later on while he was still in Corinth, he wrote the Thessalonians another letter to answer more of their questions. We have both of those letters called *First Thessalonians* and *Second Thessalonians*. They are gifts from God to us.

In his letters, Paul confirms to them and to us that indeed **Christ is our returning Lord**. We can be joyful about the news that He is coming back for us. And, we can live in a way that fills our hearts with joy while waiting.

THE ANSWER: CHRIST IS OUR RETURNING LORD

What fears do you have about death and dying?

Read 1 Thessalonians 4:13-18.

Verse 13—What does Paul call the dead Christians?

Verse 14-15—Will those who had died/fallen asleep miss Jesus' return?

Verses 16—What does this verse say will happen when Jesus comes back again?

Verse 17—What does this verse say will happen when Jesus comes back again?

Verse 18—Why would this information be encouraging to Christians?

For Christians, death is like falling asleep on earth and waking up in heaven where Jesus is. Believers have hope that nonbelievers do not have. Grief is real; sadness is a normal human emotion. We miss those we love who have died. But if they are Christians, they are instantly with Jesus. We can rejoice about that.

No Christian who has died will miss Jesus' return. They will be coming with Him to get those of us who are still alive. We will rise to meet Jesus in the air. In our English translations, verse 17 uses the words "caught up" to describe Jesus coming for us. About 300 years after Jesus died, Latin translators used the word "rapturo" to translate the original Greek phrase into Latin. That's why this event has been called "The Rapture" ever since.

Read Philippians 3:20-21.

What is the promise to believers?

The Bible tells us that when Jesus returns, He will make new bodies for all believers—those still alive and those who died—new bodies like Jesus' resurrected body—sinless, never to die again. He'll take us all to heaven, where we really belong, to live with Him in our new bodies until the time is right for us to come back to live on the earth with Him.

How do you feel knowing that Christ is our returning Lord and that He is coming back for you one day?

Second Thessalonians refers to the time after the Rapture when there is great distress on the earth (commonly called "The Tribulation") until Christ returns to win victory over His enemies and set up His kingdom on earth.

We don't know when Jesus will return. But, just like you prepare for guests coming to visit, you can prepare for Jesus to come back at any time. You don't sit around doing nothing or doing bad things. And, you want them to know that you love them, are excited about knowing them, and are eager for their coming. That applies to Jesus returning, too. **Christ is our returning Lord**. We can do some things to prepare while waiting.

Read 1 Thessalonians 5:16-18. What could each phrase look like in your life?

Verse 16 "always be joyful"—

Verse 17 "never stop praying"—

Verse 18 "give thanks no matter what happens"—

Even if things aren't going our way all the time, we can still rejoice in the fact that Jesus, the Son of God, loves us individually. This rejoicing may not be easy. It does take practice, but it's good for us to try.

And continuing to pray without ceasing really helps with the joyful part when times are tough. We can take everything to God, even the bad or sad things, and we will receive His peace (Philippians 4:6-7). Now, "peace" may not sound like "joy," but it's a whole lot better than "miserable," isn't it?

Give thanks no matter what else happens—and even if being thankful isn't what you feel like at the time. You need to thank God regularly for what He did by sending Jesus for you. This will certainly contribute to your being joyful.

In Paul's letter to the Thessalonians, **Christ is our returning Lord.**

When He comes, we will receive new bodies and live forever with Him. Be joyful about that and live joyfully while waiting!

LIVING DEPENDENTLY ON CHRIST

1) Bible verse to learn:

"For the Lord himself will come down from heaven, with a loud command, with the voice of the archangel and with the trumpet call of God, and the dead in Christ will rise first. After that, we who are still alive and are left will be caught up together with

them in the clouds to meet the Lord in the air. And so we will be
with the Lord forever." (1 Thessalonians 4:16-17 NIV)

2) Response in prayer & praise:

Praise God for the hope you have that Jesus is coming again for you and that you don't have to be afraid of death.

Ask Jesus to help you be joyful, to be faithful to pray, and to be thankful while waiting for Him to return.

3) Getting to know Him more:

Spend a few minutes each day reading these wonderful letters and reflecting on how God's marvelous grace offers you a life of freedom and joy.

Read 1 Thessalonians chapter 1.

Reflect on what you read.

Read 1 Thessalonians chapter 2.

Reflect on what you read.

Read 1 Thessalonians chapter 3.

Reflect on what you read.

Read 1 Thessalonians chapter 4.

Reflect on what you read.

Read 1 Thessalonians chapter 5.

Reflect on what you read.

Optional: Read 2 Thessalonians chapters 1-3.

Reflect on what you read.

GRACE OVERFLOWING 10 — The First Letter to Timothy

"For there is one God and one mediator between God and mankind, the man Christ Jesus..." (1 Timothy 2:5 NIV)

GRACE OVERFLOWING

- ✓ In ROMANS, **Christ is our righteousness.** Every believer is equally right with God and has equal righteousness from God.

- ✓ In 1 CORINTHIANS: **Christ is the wisdom of God**, greater than any human wisdom or strength.

- ✓ In 2 CORINTHIANS: **Christ is our comforter** when we hurt.

- ✓ In GALATIANS: **Christ is our freedom from the law** of works to earn God's acceptance.

- ✓ In EPHESIANS: **Christ is the powerful head of the church.** Christ's power works **in us** to help us live God's way and **for us** to protect us from anything evil.

- ✓ In PHILIPPIANS: **Christ is the supplier of every need** of yours so that you can help others.

- ✓ In COLOSSIANS: **Christ is Lord over everything.** He is Lord over the universe, the earth, the angels, and our behavior.

- ✓ In 1 & 2 THESSALONIANS: **Christ is our returning Lord.** When He comes, we will receive new bodies and live forever with Him.

THE KEY QUESTION

When have you needed someone to represent you to someone else?

Whoever did that for you was acting as a mediator—someone who goes between two people or groups to solve a problem or settle a dispute. A professional baseball player hires an agent to act as a mediator between himself and a team that is interested in hiring him. The mediator needs to understand both sides—what the player needs and what the team needs.

The key word for this lesson is **mediator**. The questions we'll consider are, "Why do we need a mediator, and who is the best one for us?" Paul's friend Timothy needed to give the people in his church the answer to those questions.

THE PEOPLE AND THEIR NEED

Timothy was a teenager when he met Paul. You can read his story in Acts 16. His family lived in Lystra so he was a Galatian. His father was a Greek man; we know nothing of his faith. But, Timothy's mom and grandmother were faithful Jewish women who taught the Old Testament scriptures to this boy they loved so much. As the women heard Paul preach, they believed in Jesus, and so did Timothy.

Timothy may have seen Paul heal a lame man in his town. That would have been exciting! He may also have watched as an angry mob threw stones at Paul and left him for dead. Yet, he also knew Paul survived.

When Paul came back to Lystra a couple of years later on his second missionary journey, Paul invited Timothy to travel with him. What an

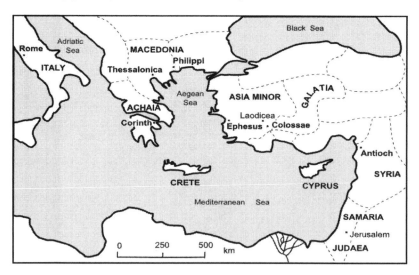

honor! Do you think Timothy might have been a little bit scared, too?

Timothy helped Paul as he preached throughout Greece—Macedonia in the north and Achaia in the south. He carried money to Paul collected by the Philippian church to care for Paul's needs in Corinth. Timothy could be trusted. During the 3 years Paul was in Ephesus teaching them about the amazing power of God, Timothy was there, too.

When Paul was in a Roman prison for two years, Timothy was right alongside him much of the time unselfishly taking care of Paul's needs. By now, Timothy was a young man of about 30 who for at least 13 years had been learning how to teach about Jesus and serve God's people well as he watched Paul do it.

Timothy was teachable! Paul thought of Timothy not only as a very faithful friend but also as his spiritual son. The one who leads you to trust Christ becomes your spiritual mother or father. Did you know that?

Hooray! Paul was finally free again. So, he and Timothy traveled to visit friends in the churches they had founded. When they got to **Ephesus**, Paul recognized some men in the church were teaching bad stuff about Jesus, saying that Jesus could not have been a man and God at the same time.

Paul wanted to go on to visit his friends in **Macedonia**, but he didn't want to leave the Ephesian church in turmoil. So, he left Timothy to teach truth to the church there while Paul went on to Macedonia. Paul thought he'd get back to Ephesus soon, but that didn't happen. He was concerned about what was going on in Ephesus, so Paul wrote a letter.

We have that letter called *First Timothy*. It is a gift from God to us. In it Paul reminded Timothy, the Ephesians and us that Jesus was fully God and fully man. He had to be both in order to be the perfect mediator for us. In First Timothy, **Christ is our mediator**. Let's see what that means.

THE ANSWER: CHRIST IS OUR MEDIATOR

Read 1 Timothy 1:11-17.

Verse 11—What was entrusted to Paul?

Verses 12—What had Jesus done for Paul?

Verse 13—For what does Paul thank Jesus?

Verse 14—What did Paul receive?

Verses 15-16—How does Paul view himself?

Verse 17—What is Paul's response to God's abundant grace toward him?

True teaching agrees with the good news that Christ Jesus came into the world to save sinners, those who have done wrong things against God's ways. Paul was thankful for this good news for himself because he was a sinner who needed God's mercy. Christ showed him that mercy and love, too.

Did Paul need someone to understand how bad he was and how much he needed help? He calls himself the worst of sinners. He couldn't help himself. He didn't know any better. Paul needed a mediator to get him out of his trouble.

Reread verse 14.

Remember that grace is "undeserved favor." The phrase, "the grace of our Lord poured out abundantly," carried the idea of overflowing.

What picture comes to mind when you read about something overflowing with abundance?

How generous is God with His grace to everyone?

Read 1 Timothy 2:3-6.

Verse 4—What does God want?

Verse 5—Who is the go-between for God and humans?

Verse 6—As the perfect man, what did Christ Jesus do for us?

Remember that the title Christ refers to Jesus as God. Notice Paul's emphasis on Jesus as a man. Do you think of Jesus as a man, as a human just like you are? It's easy to forget that Jesus was fully human like you are. As a man, Jesus could understand how you feel and think. He could understand your troubles and how hard it is to get yourself out of trouble, especially to get rid of the wrong things you do against God. He can have compassion on your helplessness. Isn't that wonderful news!

In 1 Timothy 2:5 (NIV), Jesus is called our **mediator**. A mediator helps to solve a dispute between two persons. We were separated from our God because of our sin. Jesus took that sin upon Himself—became the bridge for us to have a relationship with God. No one else, nothing else can ever do that for us—not a parent, a boss, a judge, or a pastor—only Jesus Christ, who was fully human and fully God. Because He was both, He could represent each side perfectly. Isn't God's plan wonderful?

In 1 Timothy, **Christ Jesus is the mediator** between us and God. No man or woman can do that for you. Christ is the perfect mediator between God and mankind. As mediator, Jesus understands our needs and the best way for God to take care of our needs.

Read Hebrews 4:15-16.

What can you do when you are weak and hurting (verse 16)?

When can you go to Him? How often?

What do you receive from Him?

How should that make you feel?

When you are weak and hurting, you can go directly to Jesus and tell Him all about it. You can go to Him any time and as often as you need it. You will receive grace and mercy in your time of need. That's a promise! And, you should feel thankful for receiving mercy and help just like Paul was thankful for Christ Jesus showing him mercy when he needed it.

Now to the King eternal, immortal, invisible, the only God, be honor and glory forever and ever. Amen. (1 Timothy 1:17)

LIVING DEPENDENTLY ON CHRIST

1) Bible verse to learn:

"For there is one God and one mediator between God and mankind, the man Christ Jesus..." (1 Timothy 2:5 NIV)

2) Response in prayer & praise:

Where are you hurting today? Where are you feeling weak? Go to Jesus now and tell Him all about it. Let Him pour out His grace on you abundantly.

Respond by joining Paul in his response of praise to God (1 Timothy 1:17) for His marvelous plan of grace.

3) Getting to know Him more:

Spend a few minutes each day reading this wonderful letter and reflecting on how God's marvelous grace offers you a life of freedom and joy.

Read 1 Timothy chapter 1.

Reflect on what you read.

Read 1 Timothy chapter 2.

Reflect on what you read.

Read 1 Timothy chapter 3.

Reflect on what you read.

Read 1 Timothy chapter 4.

Reflect on what you read.

Read 1 Timothy chapter 5.

Reflect on what you read.

Read 1 Timothy chapter 6.

Reflect on what you read.

GRACE OVERFLOWING 11 The Second Letter to Timothy

*"Now there is in store for me the **crown** of righteousness, which the Lord, the righteous Judge, will award to me on that day— and not only to me, but also to all who have longed for his appearing." (2 Timothy 4:8 NIV)*

GRACE OVERFLOWING

- ✓ In ROMANS, **Christ is our righteousness.** Every believer is equally right with God and has equal righteousness from God.

- ✓ In 1 CORINTHIANS, **Christ is the wisdom of God**, greater than any human wisdom or strength.

- ✓ In 2 CORINTHIANS, **Christ is our comforter** when we hurt.

- ✓ In GALATIANS, **Christ is our freedom from the law** of works to earn God's acceptance.

- ✓ In EPHESIANS, **Christ is the powerful head of the church.** Christ's power works **in us** to help us live God's way and **for us** to protect us from anything evil.

- ✓ In PHILIPPIANS, **Christ is the supplier of every need** of yours so that you can help others.

- ✓ In COLOSSIANS, **Christ is Lord over everything.** He is Lord over the universe, the earth, the angels, and our behavior.

- ✓ In 1 & 2 THESSALONIANS, **Christ is our returning Lord.** When He comes, we will receive new bodies and live forever with Him.

- ✓ In 1 TIMOTHY, **Christ is our mediator.** As mediator, Jesus understands our needs and the best way for God to take care of our needs.

THE KEY QUESTION

Do you like to give gifts? What do you like best about giving gifts to someone? How do you go about picking out what you want to give? Are you a cheerful giver, or do you resent having to bring a gift to someone? What kinds of things can you give that don't cost money? Do those gifts still cost you something like time, effort, and creativity? What's the best gift you have given to someone?

The key word for our lesson today is **giving**. The questions to ask are, "Who is the best giver, what does He give to us, and how can we be givers like He is?" Some of Paul's friends needed to know the answer to those questions.

THE PEOPLE AND THEIR NEED

Remember that Paul loved Timothy as a son and a friend. After Paul's release from his first Roman imprisonment, he and Timothy traveled to visit friends in the churches they had founded. When they got to **Ephesus**, Paul left Timothy to teach truth to the church there while Paul went on to **Macedonia**. Paul thought he'd get back to Ephesus soon, but that didn't happen. So he wrote the letter called First Timothy.

Paul traveled for a while longer, but then he was arrested again and sent to **Rome**. This time Paul was thrown into a cold dungeon, and he knew that he would soon die! Paul had already appeared once before the wicked Roman emperor Nero, and he expected to be tried again. Nero had become more wicked in his hatred for Christians.

Paul felt very lonely because many of his friends had left him. At this time, only his doctor friend Luke (the writer of *Luke* and *Acts*) was still

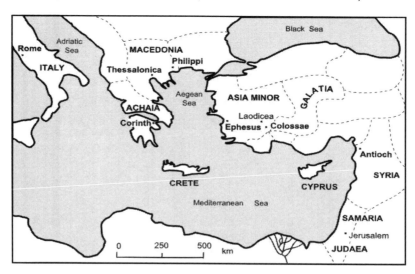

with him in Rome. Other friends were taking care of the churches Paul had founded, including Timothy who was still pastoring the church at **Ephesus**. Paul knew God was with him still, even in prison. He wrote another letter to Timothy, the last one he wrote that we have in our Bibles. Paul asked Timothy to come right away and bring his coat and scrolls he left behind in Ephesus. Paul was not sure Timothy would get to Rome before Paul was killed. A very sad time!

This letter contains Paul's last words of encouragement to Timothy and warnings that Nero's hatred of Christians would cause many believers to suffer. We have this letter called *Second Timothy*. It is a gift from God to us.

In his letter, Paul reminds Timothy to stand firm on the truth he had heard from Paul. Don't let the bad teachers win. Don't give up because of suffering. The Holy Spirit would be his continual helper and guide. And, Jesus Christ rewards those who are faithful to Him. He gives many good gifts, including crowns. Yes, I said crowns. In Second Timothy, **Christ is the giver of crowns**. Let's find out what that means for us.

THE ANSWER: CHRIST IS THE GIVER OF CROWNS

Read 2 Timothy 2:1-6, 15.

According to verse 2, how does the true message get passed on?

According to verses 4-6, what do the soldier, athlete, and farmer have in common?

According to verse 15, what are we supposed to do?

Pastors and church leaders are to teach trustworthy people who can teach others, also. This is called disciplemaking—making disciples for Jesus. As individual followers of Christ, we are to do our best to please God and to teach truth correctly. Paul continues to encourage Timothy to keep doing what is right and keep teaching truth even if some people who hated Christians would try to stop his teaching what the Bible says.

Read 2 Timothy 4:7-8.

Does Paul feel that his life has been faithful to the God he serves?

What is waiting for him?

Who will give it to him? [NOTE: Some translations use the word "award" rather than "give" in verse 8, but it means the same thing.]

Who else will receive a crown?

Does that include you?

In Second Timothy, **Christ is the giver of crowns**. Christ is a giver. In fact, He is the best giver of all, including the giving of crowns.

Read 1 Peter 5:1-4.

What crown does the Lord Jesus give?

To whom and for what reason?

Read James 1:12.

What crown does the Lord Jesus give to everyone who loves Him?

Some crowns are rewards to believers who have worked hard to please the Lord Jesus as in the "Crown of Righteousness" and the "Crown of Glory." Other crowns are given to every believer as in the "Crown of Life."

But, we've learned in Paul's other letters that Christ is a giver not only of crowns but also of many other things to those who trust in Him. To all believers, Christ gives forgiveness of all sin, salvation, and eternal life. We have also learned that Christ provides a relationship between God and man (1 Timothy) that gives freedom from the law so we can choose to please God (Galatians). He is the supplier of every need (Philippians) who gives protection and Holy Spirit power to live a life that pleases God (Ephesians) as we change our behavior (Colossians).

Christ gives us spiritual wisdom (1 Corinthians), comfort (2 Corinthians), righteousness (Romans), and a new body when He returns (1 Thessalonians). We will soon learn that He also gives us hope (Titus) and new hearts (Philemon).

Jesus Christ is the best giver! He rewards those who are faithful to Him.

Christ is the best giver! We can follow His example and be givers, also. But, we sometimes get to thinking about ourselves too much and don't want to be givers.

Read 2 Timothy 3:1-5.

How does Paul describe the different types of people who are living to be takers rather than givers?

Yikes! That sounds pretty bad, doesn't it? Do you know anyone like that now?

Look at Paul's warning in verse 5. The New International Readers Version puts it this way, "Teach the people not to follow their example!"

What choices must you make to not follow their examples?

Read 2 Timothy 3:14-17.

How do you stay on track in following the right examples?

Does God want you to be a giver because you have to or because you love Him and want to please Him in gratitude for what He has done for you?

What do you think you will do with the crown Christ gives you when you get to heaven some day?

Read Revelation 4:10-11.

Some think the 24 elders represents all believers in the Church. They give back their crowns, laying them at Jesus' feet. Why do you think they do that?

Jesus Christ is the best giver! He rewards those who are faithful to Him. He gives many good gifts, including crowns. In Second Timothy, **Christ is the giver of crowns**.

LIVING DEPENDENTLY ON CHRIST

1) **Bible verse to learn:**

"Now there is in store for me the crown of righteousness, which the Lord, the righteous Judge, will award to me on that day— and not only to me, but also to all who have longed for his appearing." (2 Timothy 4:8 NIV)

2) Response in prayer & praise:

Thank Jesus for what He gives to you. Ask Jesus for a heart that wants to give to others as Jesus has given to you. Ask Him to help you stick to the truth of God's Word even when others do not.

3) Getting to know Him more:

Spend a few minutes each day reading this wonderful letter and reflecting on how God's marvelous grace offers you a life of freedom and joy.

Read 2 Timothy chapter 1.

Reflect on what you read.

Read 2 Timothy chapter 2.

Reflect on what you read.

Read 2 Timothy chapter 3.

Reflect on what you read.

Read 2 Timothy chapter 4.

Reflect on what you read.

The Letter to Titus

*"That's how we should live as we wait for the **blessed hope** God has given us. We are waiting for Jesus Christ to appear in all his glory. He is our great God and Savior." (Titus 2:13 NIRV)*

GRACE OVERFLOWING

✓ In ROMANS, **Christ is our righteousness.** Every believer is equally right with God and has equal righteousness from God.

✓ In 1 CORINTHIANS, **Christ is the wisdom of God**, greater than any human wisdom or strength.

✓ In 2 CORINTHIANS, **Christ is our comforter** when we hurt.

✓ In GALATIANS, **Christ is our freedom from the law** of works to earn God's acceptance.

✓ In EPHESIANS, **Christ is the powerful head of the church.** Christ's power works **in us** to help us live God's way and **for us** to protect us from anything evil.

✓ In PHILIPPIANS, **Christ is the supplier of every need** of yours so that you can help others.

✓ In COLOSSIANS, **Christ is Lord over everything.** He is Lord over the universe, the earth, the angels, and our behavior.

✓ In 1 & 2 THESSALONIANS, **Christ is our returning Lord.** When He comes, we will receive new bodies and live forever with Him.

✓ In 1 TIMOTHY, **Christ is our mediator.** As mediator, Jesus understands our needs and the best way for God to take care of our needs.

✓ In 2 TIMOTHY, **Christ is the giver of crowns.** He rewards those who are faithful to Him.

THE KEY QUESTION

What is hope? Your answer depends on your perspective. The kind of hope that the world offers is generally the wishful thinking kind where someone is not sure they will get what they want or need but "hopes" they will. Biblical hope is the **confident expectation** of something that will definitely take place because it is based on God's promises.

When do you need hope?

What happens when you lose hope?

The key word for our lesson today is **hope**. You need hope whenever you are facing something tough to do, when you are sad and/or when you can't see the end. The result of losing hope is discouragement. The questions to ask are, "What is hope in the Bible, and how does hope affect our lives?" Paul's friend Titus needed to give the people in the churches on the island of Crete the answer to those questions.

THE PEOPLE AND THEIR NEED

During Paul's first missionary journey, a young man named Titus heard Paul preach about Jesus. Titus was a Gentile—he had not grown up worshiping the God of the Bible. As he listened to Paul, Titus' heart responded to the message, and he believed in Jesus. Paul brought him to Jerusalem to show the apostles and other Jewish believers how a Gentile could love God just as much as they did. Titus represented all the other non-Jewish people who became Christians and were completely accepted by God through their faith in Jesus Christ—like most of us! Hooray!

Titus continued to travel with Paul on missionary journeys, helping in the work of sharing the gospel. During the 3 years Paul was in Ephesus teaching them about the amazing power of God (third

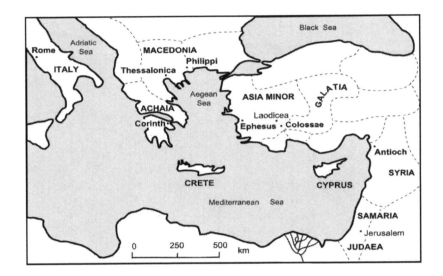

journey), Titus was there. Then, Paul sent him to Corinth to help that church with its work. Paul thought of Titus not only as a very faithful friend but also as his spiritual son because he had led him to trust Christ.

After Paul was released from the Roman prison where he had been for two years, he and Titus traveled to the island of **Crete** (see the map). The people, called Cretans, were known to be very rough people who were liars, were lazy, and loved to eat and argue with one another. Paul and Titus taught them about their need for God and the good news about Jesus. God was certainly powerful enough to change their hearts and their behavior. Soon there were enough believers to start churches in several towns.

Paul wanted to go visit the church in **Corinth** so he left Titus to continue teaching the new Christians and to appoint church leaders for each new church. When someone came to replace him in Crete, Titus met Paul in western Macedonia and continued the missionary work northward into what is now Albania. The gospel was spreading farther into Europe.

While on the island of Crete, Titus was a busy man as he cared for all the new Cretan believers, especially because the people just didn't know how to do what is good in God's eyes. Paul knew Titus needed some encouragement and reminders of what was important to teach the people. So, Paul wrote a letter to Titus. We have that letter called

Titus. It is a gift from God to us. In it Paul reminded Titus, the Cretans, and us that **Christ is our hope** for any kind of life that pleases God. Our hope in Christ sets us free from the bad things we used to do and teaches us to do what is good. Let's find out more about this hope we have in Christ.

THE ANSWER: CHRIST IS OUR BLESSED HOPE

Read Titus 2:11-12.

Paul says God's grace teaches us to say "no" to godless ways. What do you think are "godless ways"? See also 3:3.

If we say "no" to godless ways, we must say "yes" to something else. What does Paul say in the rest of verse 12?

Who gives you power to live this way—your own strength or the Holy Spirit living inside you?

Godless ways are things that go against God's way of living a life that pleases Him. We are to say "no" to godless ways and "yes" to doing what is right in today's world. The Holy Spirit living inside of us is the only way we can consistently do what is right. Don't forget that. Jesus wants us to live in dependence on His Spirit inside of us to be able to live the kind of life that pleases God.

Read Titus 2:13.

What is one promise given to us in this verse?

What is Christ called in this verse?

In Titus, **Christ is our blessed hope.** The word "hope" in the Bible is the confident expectation of something that will definitely happen because it's based on God's promises and faithfulness. It has been promised to you, it is good, and you know it will happen. In Titus 2:13, the promise is that Christ is going to appear in all his glory. He is coming back. We will see Him at some point in the future—guaranteed. That's hope we have in Christ. Let's see some of the other good things we have.

Read Titus 2:14.

What has Christ already done for us?

For what purpose?

Read Titus 3:4-6.

What has Christ already done for us?

How are our lives renewed?

Read Titus 3:7.

What other hope do we have?

We have already been set free from doing bad things in order to do what is good. Our sins have been washed away permanently. We've been given new life now by God's Holy Spirit who lives inside us from the moment we believe in Jesus. That life lasts forever. The Spirit gives us power to live the kind of life that pleases God. We've been adopted as God's children. All these things have been provided for us by Christ who is our hope.

Knowing God's promise that all those good things will happen to you, how does that make you feel?

In Titus, **Christ is our blessed hope**. The word "blessed" means "happy." We can be truly happy in our hope because we know all those things promised to us will happen. Hope is God's gift to us.

Remember that hope is the confident expectation of something that will definitely happen.

We have this blessed hope in Christ. It can never be taken away from us. Knowing this can help us in two ways:

- We can look at life as an **adventure with God** because the best is yet to come for us.

- We can let God's Spirit give us a longing to do what is good.

Let's look at each one of those.

First, looking at life as an adventure with God. What do you think would happen if you began each day by asking, "What new adventure do you have for me today, O God?" How would that affect the way you looked at your day?

Second, longing to do what is good. We will long to please God—not because we have to do good things but because we are so thankful for what God has done for us that we want to do what pleases Him. We can be teachable—letting God's Spirit teach us how to say "no" to godless ways and "yes" to doing what is right while we are waiting for Jesus to come back.

Where do you need to say "no" and "yes" in your life?

Who gives us the hope to live a life of adventure with God and learn to do what is good?

In Titus, **Christ is our blessed hope**—the confident expectation of something that will definitely happen because God has promised it to us. That kind of hope will never disappoint.

LIVING DEPENDENTLY ON CHRIST

1) **Bible verse to learn:**

"That's how we should live as we wait for the blessed hope God has given us. We are waiting for Jesus Christ to appear in all his glory. He is our great God and Savior." (Titus 2:13 NIRV)

2) **Response in prayer & praise:**

This time respond through any creative means you choose (journaling, prayer, poem, drawing, painting, song) to illustrate what you have learned from this lesson about Christ being your hope. An extra page is added at the end of this lesson for you. This will be your praise to Him today.

3) Getting to know Him more:

Spend a few minutes each day reading this wonderful letter and reflecting on how God's marvelous grace offers you a life of freedom and joy.

Read Titus chapter 1.

Reflect on what you read.

Read Titus chapter 2.

Reflect on what you read.

Read Titus chapter 3.

Reflect on what you read.

GRACE OVERFLOWING 13 — The Letter to Philemon

*"**Renew** my heart. We know that Christ is the one who really renews it." (Philemon 20b NIRV)*

GRACE OVERFLOWING

- ✓ In ROMANS, **Christ is our righteousness.** Every believer is equally right with God and has equal righteousness from God.

- ✓ In 1 CORINTHIANS, **Christ is the wisdom of God**, greater than any human wisdom or strength.

- ✓ In 2 CORINTHIANS, **Christ is our comforter** when we hurt.

- ✓ In GALATIANS, **Christ is our freedom from the law** of works to earn God's acceptance.

- ✓ In EPHESIANS, **Christ is the powerful head of the church.** Christ's power works **in us** to help us live God's way and **for us** to protect us from anything evil.

- ✓ In PHILIPPIANS, **Christ is the supplier of every need** of yours so that you can help others.

- ✓ In COLOSSIANS, **Christ is Lord over everything.** He is Lord over the universe, the earth, the angels, and our behavior.

- ✓ In 1 & 2 THESSALONIANS, **Christ is our returning Lord.** When He comes, we will receive new bodies and live forever with Him.

- ✓ In 1 TIMOTHY, **Christ is our mediator.** As mediator, Jesus understands our needs and the best way for God to take care of our needs.

- ✓ In 2 TIMOTHY, **Christ is the giver of crowns.** He rewards those who are faithful to Him.

- ✓ In TITUS, **Christ is our blessed hope.** We can look at life as an adventure with God because the best is yet to come for us.

THE KEY QUESTION

Think about a time when someone wronged you. How long did you stay wounded? What did it take (or would it take) to bring about reconciliation? How hard was it to forgive that person?

The key word for our lesson today is **forgiveness**. The question to ask is, "How do I really forgive someone who has wronged me?" Some of Paul's friends needed to know the answer to that question.

THE PEOPLE AND THEIR NEED

Paul looked across the room of his **Roman** prison at the young man, Onesimus. How dear he was to Paul! The young slave had stolen some money from his master in **Colossae** and run away. Somehow he ended up in Rome and met Paul. Though Paul was chained to a Roman guard, people could come and visit him, even stay with him.

Somehow Onesimus found his way to Paul, Paul told the runaway slave about Jesus, and Onesimus trusted Christ to take away his sins. Paul became his spiritual father, teaching him and loving him as a Christian son. Onesimus learned to love Christ Jesus and received a renewed heart.

As much as Paul wanted this young man to stay near him, he knew that Onesimus should return to Philemon, his owner, and seek forgiveness for stealing the money and for running away. Philemon

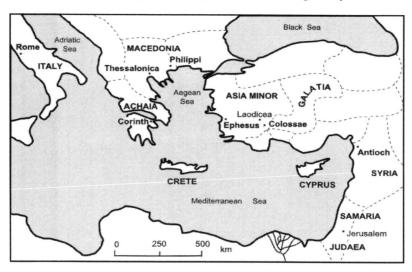

was a fairly rich man who owned slaves. It was common for people to have slaves. One of every two persons in the Roman Empire was a slave. Every large Roman household had them. Slaves were not free to do whatever they wanted but had to do whatever their owner said. And, any slave who ran away could be killed. Paul certainly didn't want that to happen to his son Onesimus. Paul had to trust Jesus with Onesimus' safety.

We don't know if Paul ever met Philemon though Paul seemed to know of him well enough to appreciate him as a Christian brother and a leader of the church in **Colossae**. Christ had renewed Philemon's heart from being a sinner separated from God to being completely forgiven.

Now, Philemon the slave owner and Onesimus the runaway slave were Christian brothers. Would Onesimus have the courage to return to his master, or would he run away again? Would Philemon forgive Onesimus for stealing money and running away, or would he have Onesimus killed?

Well, Paul sent Onesimus back to Philemon. It was the right thing to do. And, he sent a letter along with Onesimus. We have that letter called *Philemon*. It is a gift from God to us. *Philemon* is the shortest of Paul's letters, more like a postcard. It's also the most personal.

In his letter, Paul reminded Philemon and us that **Christ is the renewer of hearts.** Christ had renewed Paul's heart many years before. He had renewed Philemon's heart when he heard the gospel message and believed. Christ had renewed Onesimus' heart. A renewed heart is grateful for the forgiveness received through God's grace and wants to be a "grace giver" to others. Let's find out how that works.

THE ANSWER: CHRIST IS THE RENEWER OF HEARTS

Philemon has only 1 chapter so we just use verse numbers. Since it is so short, we'll read most of it to get the whole story.

Read Philemon 1-2.

What information is given about Philemon?

Read Philemon 4-7.

In Verses 4-5: What kind of Christian was Philemon?

In verse 7: Referring to what Philemon has done for God's people, Paul says that he has "renewed their hearts." [NOTE: the NIV says "refreshed the hearts of the saints."] What do you think that means to renew or refresh their hearts?

Read Philemon 8-11.

What did Paul do instead of ordering Philemon to forgive Onesimus?

Paul calls Philemon a dear friend who was working for the gospel. A church met in his home. Apphia and Archippus are probably his wife and son who are fellow believers. Philemon was faithful and loving as he took care of the needs of the church there in Colossae, encouraging the people and giving them hope. Notice how Paul says he was in prison and that Onesimus was his spiritual son and a fellow believer. By not ordering Philemon to forgive Onesimus, Paul made him think about it and appealed to him on the basis of love.

What would be the advantage to both of them if Philemon forgave Onesimus out of love and respect for Christ and Paul rather than doing so just because he felt forced to do it?

Read Philemon 12-16.

In verses 12-14, how does Paul show respect for Philemon's authority as a slave owner?

According to verses 15-16, how has the slave-master relationship changed?

Paul knows Philemon has the right to make all decisions regarding Onesimus. So, he sends Onesimus back rather than assuming it's okay for him to stay with Paul. But, now Onesimus is more than a slave. He's a Christian brother. That changes everything in his relationship with Philemon.

Read Philemon 17-22.

In verse 17, Paul asked Philemon to welcome Onesimus back. What might be the opposite of welcoming him?

In verses 18-19, Paul offered to pay anything Onesimus owed to Philemon. Hmmm. Did Paul steal the money?

Who else do you know took the consequences for someone else's bad behavior?

Jesus died on the cross for our sins, not for his own. Paul repeated Jesus' example of someone who substitutes himself for another. Paul didn't have to pay what Onesimus owes, but he offered to do it to help heal the relationship between Onesimus and Philemon. Christ healed our relationship with God when He died on the cross for our sins even though He never sinned.

In Philemon, **Christ is the renewer of hearts.** In verse 20, Paul says,

"Renew my heart. We know that Christ is the one who really renews it (NIRV). "

What does it mean to renew something?

Renewing may involve restoring a relationship or repairing something broken so that it works well again. Making something like new again.

How does Christ renew our hearts?

Read Philemon 23-25.

In verse 25, Paul writes, "May the grace of the Lord Jesus Christ be with your spirit." What does Paul want Philemon to remember about his own life?

Notice that Paul calls Jesus **Lord** 5 times in this short letter. Jesus is Philemon's king and master as He is our king and master. Paul is reminding Philemon that he has received forgiveness through grace overflowing to him from Jesus who is his Lord. Because Philemon has received grace from his Lord Jesus, Philemon should, therefore, be a "grace giver" to Onesimus.

Christ calls us to be grace givers to others as we have received grace from Him.

What do you think it means to be a "grace giver"?

Read Ephesians 4:32.

How can you be a "grace giver" in your life?

A grace-giver is kind and tenderhearted, forgiving others as Christ has forgiven us. A grace-giver does not hold grudges and works at renewing relationships rather than being continually angry with someone.

What relationships in your life need renewing?

In Philemon, **Christ is the renewer of hearts,** making us right with God so our relationship with God is no longer broken. He forgives us completely, gives us new hearts and fills our hearts with joy. Christ gives us His grace so that we can then give grace to others, following His own example. A renewed heart is grateful for the forgiveness received through God's grace and wants to be a "grace giver" to others.

Living Dependently on Christ

1) Bible verse to learn:

"Renew my heart. We know that Christ is the one who really renews it." (Philemon 20b NIRV)

2) Response in prayer & praise:

Ask Jesus, as the renewer of your heart, to help you be a grace-giver to your friends and family members.

3) Getting to know Him more:

Spend a few minutes reading this wonderful letter and reflecting on how God's marvelous grace offers you a life of freedom and joy.

Read all of Philemon again.

Reflect on what you read.

A Quick Look at Paul's Letters

Letters to churches (city)	Year written	Where written	When Paul visited	Christ in the Letter
Romans (Rome)	57-58	In Corinth during Paul's 3rd missionary journey	After 3rd journey when Paul was arrested and brought to Rome as a prisoner under house arrest	Christ is our righteousness.
1st Corinthians (Corinth)	55-56	In Ephesus during Paul's 3rd missionary journey	During 2nd missionary journey	Christ is the wisdom of God.
2nd Corinthians (Corinth)	55-56	In Macedonia during Paul's 3rd missionary journey	During 2nd missionary journey	Christ is our comforter
Galatians (region of Galatia)	49	After 1st missionary journey when Paul returned to Antioch	Traveled through region on all 3 missionary journeys	Christ is our freedom from the law.
Ephesians (Ephesus)	61	During house imprisonment in Rome after 3rd missionary journey	During 2nd and 3rd missionary journeys	Christ is the powerful head of the Church.
Philippians (Philippi)	61	During house imprisonment in Rome after 3rd missionary journey	During 2nd and 3rd missionary journeys	Christ is the supplier of every need.

Colossians (Colossae)	61	During house imprisonment in Rome after 3rd missionary journey	None known	Christ is Lord over everything.
1st and 2nd Thessalonians (Thessalonica)	51	In Corinth during Paul's 2nd missionary journey	During 2nd missionary journey	Christ is our returning Lord.
Letters to individuals	**Year written**	**Where written**	**When Paul met him**	**Christ in the Letter**
1st Timothy (in Ephesus)	63-66	During Paul's 5 years of freedom after his 1st Roman imprisonment	Converted by Paul in Galatia during 1st journey; accompanied Paul on 2nd and 3rd journeys	Christ is our mediator.
2nd Timothy (in Ephesus)	67	During 2nd imprisonment in Rome just before his execution	Converted by Paul in Galatia during 1st journey; accompanied Paul on 2nd and 3rd journeys	Christ is the giver of crowns.
Titus (in Crete)	63-66	During Paul's 5 years of freedom after his 1st Roman imprisonment	Converted by Paul; accompanied Paul and Barnabas to Jerusalem on 2nd journey	Christ is our blessed hope.
Philemon (in Colossae)	61	During house imprisonment in Rome after 3rd missionary journey	Friend of Paul whose slave, Onesimus, had run away and been converted by Paul	Christ is the renewer of hearts.

Graceful Beginnings Series
FOR NEW-TO-THE-BIBLE CHRISTIANS

Designed for anyone new to the Bible. First steps for new Christians. Basic lessons introducing truths about God. Simple terms that are easily understood. Where you can start studying the Bible for yourself.

A Fresh Start

The first book in the series, laying a good foundation of truth for you to grasp and apply to your life.

Painting the Portrait of Jesus

Study the "I Am" statements of Jesus from the gospel of John that reveal who Jesus is and why you can trust Him.

The God You Can Know

Study the wonderful attributes of God so you can know Him as your loving Father.

Grace Overflowing

An overview of Paul's letters and how Christ is presented in each one as the answer to your every need.

For more information about *Graceful Beginnings* books, including new releases, visit **www.joyfulwalkpress.com**.

JOYFUL WALK PRESS